T0110884

Praise For

Waiting for a Miracle

Inspiring new author, Julianne King, has written a book that has the potential to change lives when read and taken to heart. Throughout the years that I have known Julianne, I have watched her, time and time again, gain and sustain victory as she applied the principles that God taught her. In fact, I prodded and poked Julianne to write this book, absolutely believing that what God had given her needed to be shared.

Julianne's chapter titled "Keep No Record" (chapter 4) is so important that I once told her that everyone in the world needed to receive the vital revelation gleaned from her insight! She shows how doable and rewarding it is to walk without offense as she tells of her own personal struggles and victories.

I enjoyed the many illustrations and stories throughout this book that created aha moments for me. Several statements were copied into my personal journal to be remembered and applied. You will not only enjoy this book, but Julianne's six-point plan will put tools in your hands, hope in your heart, and help transform your mind while building your confidence in God's goodness. *Waiting for a Miracle* will inspire you and the time you invest in reading this book will yield a lifetime of miracles!

Linda Anderson, author and founder of
His Way Ministries International

"Give yourself permission to practice hearing and obeying the voice of the Lord. Don't worry about always getting it right." Thank you, Jesus! Finally, someone who understands that God is more concerned about the process than about perfection! If you don't have it all figured out, if you sometimes feel inadequate, or if you're still waiting for your miracle to come to pass, then do I have a book for you. *Waiting for a Miracle* is exactly what this world needs right now.

Julianne writes from a place of humility and vulnerability but also from a position of power and purpose. Like a close friend who has permission to speak into your life, this book might ruffle a few of your pretty feathers, but it also has the potential to teach you how to use those wings to fly. Apply what you read, and the only outcome will be activating the power and beauty of Heaven over your life.

Toby Bowker, pastor of The House San Diego
and founder of Kingdom Men Ministries

Waiting *FOR A* Miracle

UNSHAKABLE FAITH IN SEASONS OF WAITING

Julianne King

authorHOUSE®

AuthorHouse™
1663 Liberty Drive
Bloomington, IN 47403
www.authorhouse.com
Phone: 833-262-8899

© *2021 Julianne King. All rights reserved.*

No part of this book may be reproduced, stored in
a retrieval system, or transmitted by any means
without the written permission of the author.

Published by AuthorHouse 02/04/2021

ISBN: 978-1-6655-1319-7 (sc)
ISBN: 978-1-6655-1318-0 (e)

Library of Congress Control Number: 2021900335

Print information available on the last page.

Any people depicted in stock imagery provided by Getty Images are
models, and such images are being used for illustrative purposes only.
Certain stock imagery © Getty Images.

The Cover Art credit goes to Dawson King
Credit for the author photo is Raquel King Photography

This book is printed on acid-free paper.

Because of the dynamic nature of the Internet, any web
addresses or links contained in this book may have changed
since publication and may no longer be valid. The views
expressed in this work are solely those of the author and do
not necessarily reflect the views of the publisher, and the
publisher hereby disclaims any responsibility for them.

New Living Translation (NLT)
Holy Bible, New Living Translation, copyright © 1996, 2004, 2015
by Tyndale House Foundation. Used by permission of Tyndale House
Publishers, Inc., Carol Stream, Illinois 60188. All rights reserved.

New American Bible (Revised Edition) (NABRE)
Scripture texts, prefaces, introductions, footnotes and cross
references used in this work are taken from the New American
Bible, revised edition © 2010, 1991, 1986, 1970 Confraternity of
Christian Doctrine, Inc., Washington, DC All Rights Reserved. No
part of this work may be reproduced or transmitted in any form or
by any means, electronic or mechanical, including photocopying,
recording, or by any information storage and retrieval system,
without permission in writing from the copyright owner.

Living Bible (TLB)
The Living Bible copyright © 1971 by Tyndale House
Foundation. Used by permission of Tyndale House Publishers
Inc., Carol Stream, Illinois 60188. All rights reserved.

The Passion Translation (TPT)
The Passion Translation®. Copyright © 2017 by
BroadStreet Publishing® Group, LLC.
Used by permission. All rights reserved. thePassionTranslation.com

New King James Version (NKJV)
Scripture taken from the New King James Version®. Copyright ©
1982 by Thomas Nelson. Used by permission. All rights reserved.

English Standard Version (ESV)
The Holy Bible, English Standard Version. ESV® Text
Edition: 2016. Copyright © 2001 by Crossway Bibles,
a publishing ministry of Good News Publishers.

Dedication

To my pastor, my mentor, and most of all, my friend-Linda Anderson. By faith, you spoke this book into existence years before I believed it was possible. May it free His people, For the Kingdom!

Contents

Acknowledgments

I am so grateful for my pastors and church family. You are living examples of "calling those things that are not as though they are." I learned at Horizon, by your faithful example, the value of every concept mentioned in this book. Your posture of expectant faith and uncompromising obedience has opened the door for abundant miracles in my life. Oh, that everyone could attend such an amazing church!

A huge "thank you" to my tribe—twelve faithful women whom I get to call friends—for spending your summer daring to believe that Heaven had a miracle just for you. I am honored to have been on this adventure with you. I hope you see yourself in the pages of this book. Your input was invaluable.

To my kids, I want to tell you that your encouragement means the world to me. Thank you for not doubting the value of what I had to say, even in the seasons when I struggled to walk it out. God has so many miracles for you—more than you can ask for or imagine.

To my husband, I know that getting this book from my head, to my heart, and onto paper was not a journey for the faint of heart. Your words of praise were most treasured because you knew, all too well, what it cost. Standing side by side, as we declared Jesus Christ as the Lord of our lives all those years ago has been my greatest miracle ever.

To my Lord, Savior, and Friend- sometimes we strolled hand in hand, sometimes I followed kicking and screaming, and sometimes You carried me. But not for a moment was I forsaken. This girl knows, without a doubt, that you are the God of miracles. All of my days, I will declare, "One moment with you changes everything!"

Foreword

Before we begin this grand adventure, we need to unpack some truths so that you have a firm foundation to stand on when the enemy comes to steal your promise. A sure, firm place to stand as you lift your shield and wield your sword is vital for your survival and advancement into the land of fulfilled promises.

Since this book is titled *Waiting for a Miracle*, let's start by defining the word *miracle*. The Oxford Dictionary of Phrase and Fable defines a miracle as a "surprising and welcome event that is not explainable by natural or scientific laws and is therefore considered to be the work of a divine agency." Wow. Let that sink in.

That leads us to the second layer in our foundation. If you are believing for a miracle, you will need to acknowledge, early and often, that worldly wisdom is not going to provide you with any helpful instruction. The Divine will almost always conflict with the practical.

> Don't let anyone capture you with empty philosophies and high-sounding nonsense that come from human thinking and from the spiritual powers of this world, rather than from Christ. For in Christ lives all the fullness of God in human body. (Colossians 2:8–9 NLT)

You must align yourself with the indisputable fact that what you will be asked to do will appear as foolishness to the world. Having one foot grounded in God's Word and one in the world's reality will leave you as easy prey for the enemy. He will seek to manipulate your senses and cause you to base your truth on your feelings instead of on the Word of God. Trust me. I know personally that this is a recipe for depression and failure.

During a particularly trying season, the Lord dropped this truth into my spirit. It has been a plumb line for me ever since. "God's Word trumps reality *every time!*" (emphasis God's).

Read it again.

Settle it deep in your spirit and resolve to know, beyond a shadow of a doubt, that God's Word is the only truth that matters. It is unshakable, indisputable, and 100 percent reliable, now and forevermore.

I love this excerpt from *Birthing the Miraculous* by Heidi Baker: "This is often how our promises from the Lord look—completely and utterly impossible!"

In laying this foundation, please keep in mind that this is not a book detailing how to get a miracle. Miracles are the gift of a loving and merciful God. Only God can give a miracle. That said, we can choose to partner with Him and be both the recipient of a miracle and the instrument that God uses to bring forth a miracle in the lives of others. We will unpack several examples in scripture where this is the case.

But here's a warning: I also believe we can stop a miracle with our words of unbelief. Is it possible that is why Zachariah was made mute until after the time of John the Baptist's birth? (see Luke 1:5–25, 57–64) His doubting words of unbelief, which he spoke when he was told the good news that Elizabeth would bare him a son, put him in opposition to the promise of God. In this instance, God overrode his physical body by silencing him.

That is not always the case.

In scripture, the Israelites were about to enter their Promised Land. As they stood in the wilderness of Paran (see Numbers 13:1–33), ten of the twelve spies came back and declared their unbelief in God's promise to give them their Promised Land. An entire generation was robbed of their miracle because of the doubting words of ten men.

My hope is that this book will help you stand fast and go forward in faith and peace as you wait for your miracle. I will give you a list of six principles, which the Lord has shown me to be present while waiting for the miracles in my life. My hope is that our time together will give you the boldness and confidence to walk full of faith in the midst of seemingly impossible odds and unlikely victories.

We *must* believe that God wants to do miraculous things in the lives of His people. How do I know this? The Word of God assures me that this is so. Every situation that we might face and need miraculous intervention from Heaven has already been written about in God's Word. The stories in the Bible are examples and not exceptions. If God did it for Moses, Abraham, Peter, Esther, Hannah, or Mary (three are mentioned), He will do it for you.

I'm reminded of the verse in Psalm 23, which says, "He has set a table before me in the presence of

Confidence to walk full of faith in the midst of seemingly impossible odds and unlikely victories.

my enemies."(vs5) My hope is that this verse will begin to take on new meaning for you.

You see, David was in that place of waiting. He

was in the valley between his current circumstances and the fulfillment of God's promise that he would be the next king of Israel. In the midst of impossible odds, as King Saul was trying to take his life, and as countless enemies surrounded him, David chose to believe and declare the words that had been spoken to him by the prophet Samuel.

Absolutely nothing was visible about his promise in that moment. Not one of his senses could discern a reality that would make the promise seem probable. But David *knew* his God. He *knew* who held his promise. In quiet confidence, he boldly declares, "HE sets a (banquet) table before me in the presence of my enemies."

That's the kind of faith the Lord has worked in my life. It's my deepest desire that this kind of faith would become your legacy too. Now let's begin. I'm full of hope that lies are going to be cast down and that joy is going to rise up, as we journey through these pages together.

1

Pray Truth

By truth, I simply mean the Word of God—period. That's it. If it doesn't agree with God's Word, then it's not the truth. I mentioned this already, but it bears repeating. God's Word trumps reality *every time!* So when I say to pray truth, I simply mean to pray God's Word.

If someone were to come up to me and ask for one thing that he or she could do to change his or her situation, I would say this, "Find out what God's Word has to say about your current situation. Write out several scriptures that speak promise to what you are going through. Then declare them prophetically until you see change. In other words, take the scriptures and declare them as a promise over what you are going through."

The Power of Declaration

God's Word is powerful, far more powerful than we give it credit for. I am often surprised by the number of Christians that I meet who are resistant or hesitant to actively partner with the Word of God to bring about His promises in their lives.

In all fairness, it's not entirely their fault. Over the years, many people have come and gone from the spotlight, who have tried to convince us that the Word of God can be manipulated to get what we want, regardless of whether it is in line with God's will for us or not. Countless books and sermons out there tell us that all we need to change our lives is a positive attitude. The result has been that the power of speaking the truth of scripture has lost the hope, peace, and promise that I believe God meant for it to have in our lives.

John 1:1–5 says it so perfectly and quite poetically.

In the beginning the Word already existed. The Word was with God, He existed in the beginning with God. God created everything through him, and nothing was created except through him. The Word gave life to everything that was created, and his life brought light to everyone. The light shines in the darkness And the darkness can never extinguish it. (NLT)

These verses are so familiar that sometimes we forget the power and hope that they offer to us. We're told in this passage that the Word is God and that it has always been. The Word is a physical expression of Jesus. It creates everything and gives it life.

This life brings light to everyone. It shines in the darkness of your situation, and the darkness cannot overcome it. Speaking God's Word, which is full of power and promise, brings light into your situation. It will overcome any dark plan or scheme of the enemy.

I'm not suggesting you just open your Bible willy-nilly, start speaking out whatever scripture your finger lands on, and expect your situation to change. Though there have been times when the first scripture that I opened my Bible to was exactly what I needed, more often than not, the scriptures that become my battle swords came in other ways.

Sometimes while doing my daily reading, a verse will jump out at me and speak directly to what I am going through. This also happens when I am doing a Bible study on a seemingly unrelated topic. God is not limited in the way that He speaks to us.

The question is this: Will we involve Him in the process? God is always about relationship. He wants to personally show us exactly what we need from His Word to bring hope, peace, and strategy.

James 1:5–6 tells us that if we need wisdom, we can go to God. If we do not doubt, He will answer us. When you spend time pursuing the Lord in the midst of your trial, He will lead you to promises in scripture that you can take as personal promises for your situation.

Strategy Revealed in the Night

This all became very real to me years ago during a very difficult season in my life. Things felt hopelessly and helplessly out of my control. They had been spiraling downward for about two years at that point. It was common for me to awaken in the middle of the night filled with fear. My thoughts swirled with worst-case scenarios. I was quick to blame the enemy for my sleepless nights. It didn't occur to me that the Lord was using the quiet hours of the night to reveal His strategy to me.

There's a verse in Psalms, and it goes like this: "The way you counsel and correct me makes me praise You more, for Your whispers in the night give me wisdom, showing me what to do next" (Psalm 16:7 TPT). It was during one of these early morning sessions that I went into my prayer closet and cried out to God in complete desperation. I begged Him to give me strategy, and this scripture jumped out at me. In that instant, I had peace because I knew that the Lord was about to bring a key.

The key came the next morning by way of an article. It was held by a magnet on the fridge in the break room where I worked. It was an article written by someone who had walked through the same trial and challenge that I was facing. That person was now walking in victory on the other side.

In it, the author explained that he and his wife had searched the scriptures for promises that spoke to their situation. They wrote thirty scriptures on note cards and began declaring them as promises over what they were going through. They were also kind enough to include the scriptures and the declarations at the end of the article.

God knows His children. At that moment, I needed it spelled out plainly. As I finished reading the article, I knew that the Lord was giving me a strategy. Filled with a hope I had not felt in years, I went home and made my own set of cards. Then I began to speak them out every night with my husband.

Just the act of coming together in agreement with God's Word was enough to see a shift in the atmosphere. Speaking out what God said kept us focused on what was possible. Each night as we prayed, we became united with the King of Glory, the Promise Keeper, and the One who lifts our heads high. The situation in front of us lost its power to stir up fear, as we were daily reminded that our God would complete the work that He had begun.

Things didn't change overnight, but we did begin to see changes. They were small at first, but things began to improve. Hope took the place of fear. What the enemy sent to divide us served instead to unite us in ways only God could do. In the past, we had focused our energy on placing blame. Now we had the Word of God to rally us and keep us focused on the solution and not the problem. Besides, blame never makes anything better.

That was about four years ago. Over the years, the Holy Spirit has prompted me to add new scriptures to the list. Others have been so fully realized that they are now declarations of thanksgiving. While not every Word has come to pass, speaking out the truth of scripture never fails to fill me with hope and bring the peace that I need to keep believing. God will always find a way to highlight the promises that we need from His Word, if we will just take the time to seek Him and believe.

Great peace and quiet confidence come from focusing our thoughts on what God says about our situations. It's a confirmation that before we even enter the valley, He knows that we will be there and makes sure to hide a promise for us in His Word. Proverbs 25:2 says, "It is God's privilege to conceal things and the king's privilege to discover them." Revelation 1:6 assures us that we are, in fact, kings and priests.

The things that used to wake me up with the kind of fear that left me breathless several times a week now rarely have the power to interrupt my night at all. We haven't seen the complete fulfillment yet, but the light shines in the darkness, and the darkness can never overcome it (see John 1:5).

This experience has set a firm belief in me of the power of God's Word. It goes so deep and is so sure that no one will ever convince me that God's Word is less than what He says it is—alive and powerful (see Hebrews 4:12 NLT).

This became my go-to for every problem and situation from that moment on. Before I ever received the six principles that would eventually form the outline for this book, I was taught the power of declaring God's Word, in faith and with passion, over my situation. Yes, God's Word can move mountains! Just the act of declaring God's Word—of seeing the depth and breadth of how much He loves and cares for us—brings a peace that gives us that deep-breath moment. It's the moment when you know God's got this.

Today, I find myself actually looking forward to

these whispers in the night. When trials and challenges come and I wake up in the night with a particular fear or worry, I know that I am being given an opportunity to get wisdom and strategy from the One who already planned my victory.

An Idea Stolen

It is a common practice for those who deal in the occult to recite spells, chants, and incantations. They do this fully expecting that in the process, they are affecting the physical world around them. I've spoken to several former self-described witches and occultists, and I am convinced that this happens more often than we believe that it does.

Yet I repeatedly find that despite my suggestion, many Christians never take the time to search the scriptures and speak God's Word over their present situation. God is the author and creator of all things. His Word carries much more power to affect change in our physical reality.

God's Word is prophecy. This brings me to the second part of praying truth that I want to share with you.

Partnering with the Prophetic

I have been blessed to have amazing, faithful, and trustworthy men and women of God who speak into my life. Prophets and the prophetic word have proven themselves reliable and dependable. The words that I have received from prophets, just as from the Word of God, have proven invaluable in my walk.

A prophetic word is a word from the Lord and delivered through the mouth of a man, woman, or in some cases even a child. All words should be tested against scripture. Once they are accepted as true, they should be declared into the atmosphere. Whether it is a word for an individual, a church, a city, or a nation, God's Word must be prayed aloud.

Once during a self-exam, I found a lump in my right breast. It had all the characteristics of the things that we are told to look for during our monthly self-checks. After showing my doctor, she too became concerned and set up a series of scans and tests for me.

Once a month, our church hosts a free healing clinic (Healing Rooms). It's a time when the community is invited to come in and receive prayer from experienced prayer-team ministers who are trained at our healing school.

Fortunately, our next Healing Rooms was set to take place the day after my trip to the doctor. I came in to receive prayer for the lump and shared the results of my visit to the doctor with a friend, who immediately prayed for me. This friend had given me several prophetic words that had brought strategy and blessing.

After praying, she told me that the Lord showed her that He had plucked the lump out of my breast and cast it into the sea. Over the next several days, I stood in faith with these words and declared them as true (see Matthew 10:41).

A few days before my first test, I couldn't find

the lump. A visit to the doctor confirmed what I already knew: the lump was no longer there. The Lord truly had reached in, plucked it out, and cast it into the sea.

I cannot overstate the importance of a true and timely word from the Lord that is spoken through a prophet. They have played such a vital part in my journey to seeing the miracles of God come to pass in my life. It has been a game changer. This has never been more true than recently.

Persistence Rewarded

For seven years, I had been waiting for a specific miracle. For seven years, I had declared promises that I had received. It seemed like every time I thought the miracle was close at hand, something would happen. Then it would seem farther away than ever. This last time was the darkest season of all.

For months, things had been mellow or calm, if you will. I wasn't walking in the promise, but hope was high, and things were steady. I'd had no obvious attack from the enemy in months. Our church had just finished an amazing conference where I saw the Lord move in power. Many people were saved, or had renewed their commitment to walk with Jesus.

A well-known and trusted prophet had come to our city and spoken words of promise over our land, which many of us had spent years believing for. I also received several fresh promises for my own miracles.

Then one day, it all came crashing in. Every bit of hope evaporated as the latest scheme of the enemy played out and stopped me in my tracks. I can't even begin to express the fear and panic that rushed in. It was truly overwhelming. In the midst of this attack, my husband lost his job, and then my father passed away.

We sent out a prayer request to a very small group of trusted prayer warriors and prophets. Without giving details that would expose anyone, we shared what was going on and asked them to pray.

The next day I received an email containing a prophetic word from one of them, a word which changed everything. This friend and prophet had taken my request to the Lord in prayer, the Lord had given him details that we had not shared in our prayer request. The Lord also gave him an encouraging word to share with us. It lined up with the scriptures that we had been declaring and the previous words that people had given us.

Hope rushed in to take the place of fear, and faith trampled upon the panic. Through one of the Lord's prophets, we received a timeline of victory for a loved one. We had been standing in faith for this person for many years. The word was personal and specific. Its effect on our spirits was immediate. A prophetic word from the Lord will do that!

I added this word to the list of scriptures that I was already praying. A very short time later, we received the breakthrough that we had been believing for. Events that I never could've planned or expected left me absolutely wrecked before the goodness of God. It took seven years. Just weeks before I thought that

I would never see the promise, but it was now being fulfilled before my eyes.

What is my point? It's always darkest before the dawn. A timely word from a trusted prophet can be the hope that you hold on to while the Lord is preparing your victory.

This was my valley moment that Psalm 23 talks about. The Lord set a table before me in the presence of my enemy. I got the chance to declare the faithfulness of the Lord and speak out His promises when there was absolutely no physical evidence to suggest that victory was close at hand.

Praying truth is a game changer!

If you do nothing else, dig into and speak out God's Word over your situation, your life, and the lives of your loved ones. If you do everything else and leave this one undone, you will not experience the peace and confidence that your Lord has made available to you.

2

Speak Life

In the last chapter, we discussed the importance of declaring the Word of God and praying truth over our situations. But what words are coming out of our mouth when we're not praying? We must be intentional about speaking life and not death to the situations that we are trusting God to move in.

> Today I have given you the choice between life and death, between blessings and curses. Now I call on Heaven and Earth to witness the choice you make. Oh that you would choose life, so that you and your descendants might live. (Deuteronomy 30:19 NLT)

We have a choice between life and death. All of Heaven waits in breathless hope, compelling us to choose life. We choose life by the words that we speak. Oh, what dreams and promises we might have blocked by speaking words of complaint and unbelief (death words)!

Moses tells us that we have a choice between life and death and consequently, a choice between a blessing and a curse. In the Oxford's English Dictionary, a blessing is defined as God's favor and protection. Consequently, a curse is defined as a solemn utterance intended to invoke a supernatural power to inflict harm or punishment on someone or something.

A solemn (earnest, thoughtful) utterance (assertion, pronouncement) intended to invoke (entreat, request). The wrong words spoken out can become a thoughtful pronouncement intended to request harm or punishment upon yourself or others!

We need to be sure that the words coming out of our mouths line up with what God says, or we may unintentionally be assisting the enemy with his destructive plans.

God's Idea and Not Ours

Over the years, I have gotten quite a bit of push back from fellow believers on this principle. The thought that our words have creative power has been called, at best, inaccurate. At worst, it has been called an advancement of new age philosophy. I'm not sure the reason this is true, except maybe that we, as a people, have become somewhat lazy in filtering our words through the lens of the Word of God.

While praying the truth of God's Word over our challenges and situations will move many mountains that have seemed otherwise immovable, speaking out words of fear can build those mountains right back up. So with the belief that God's Word is the only truth that guides us, let's see what God's Word says about the words we speak.

Before we dissect scriptures, let's look at some obvious reminders of the power of the spoken Word. God Himself created the entire universe by speaking words that brought it into existence. Jesus calmed a storm by speaking to it. He called Lazarus back from the dead with His words. Angels were dispersed from Heaven by the words of prayer that were spoken by the prophet Daniel (see Daniel 10:10–14).

The Lord stopped the sun in the sky at Joshua's spoken request. What if Joshua would've looked at his current circumstance and declared, "We're in trouble now. We will soon be out of daylight and defeated by our enemy." I imagine we would be reading about his army's defeat instead of their miraculous victory.

The following is not an exhaustive list about what the scriptures say regarding the power of our words, but they are some of my favorites. Proverbs 18:21 tells us. "Death and life are in the power of the tongue and those that partake of it will eat its fruit" (NKJV). So what kind of fruit do you like? Do you enjoy sweet and juicy or rotten and moldy fruit? It's life or death. We choose. It's life or death for our marriages, our finances, our friendships, and our children.

James 3 tells us that the tongue is untamable. It

goes so far as to say in verse 2 that if we could control our tongues, we would be perfect and could also control ourselves in every way (see James 3:1–12). Couldn't we all use the ability to control ourselves in every way?

Proverbs 15:4 tells us, "Gentle words bring life and health." Proverbs 18:4 says that a person's words can be "life-giving water." Proverbs 13:3 reminds us, "Whoever guards his mouth preserves his life."

Jesus tells us in Matthew 18:18, "Assuredly, I say to you, whatever you bind on earth will be bound in heaven, and whatever you loose on earth will be loosed in heaven." We bind and loose with the words that come out of our mouths. He goes on to state that if two or more agree on earth, it will be done in heaven. This is a reminder to use caution about the people that we share our troubles with.

Yes, our words can bring life and victory, or they can bring death. While I'm not necessarily referring to a physical death, we can kill the dreams and plans God has by habitual complaining, speaking words of doubt, and partnering with unbelief. I'm not implying that we walk around in some false utopia where we continually pretend that everything is just hunky-dory. But many of us have become way too comfortable sharing our problems with anyone who will listen.

Social media is not the place for a passive-aggressive airing of our dirty laundry or frustrations. Sharing funny, sarcastic memes about the challenges of parenting teens or the clueless inattentiveness of husbands may get likes and a few comments of sympathy, but it will not bring us closer to our victory.

In my own walk, I found myself praying with my husband over a situation one minute and then expressing to him my worries and fears in the very next breath. One day, I felt the Lord asking in my spirit, *Do you want Me to move or not?* He was showing me that I believed Him and took Him at His Word, or I did not. If I did, my words outside of my prayer time needed to line up with what I was asking Him for.

Knowing When to Speak
and When to Be Silent

So where is that balance? Obviously, we can't have the wisdom of many counselors (see Proverbs 15:22) if we are not sharing our struggles. We cannot go the extra mile and carry each other's burdens if we are not aware others have burdens to carry. We were created to do life together.

The wisdom lies in letting the Holy Spirit guide us and resisting the urge to run to the first person that we think will sympathize with us. In fact, sympathy should be the last thing that we consider when choosing a wise counselor!

I have seen more marriages destroyed by men and women seeking out others who will sympathize with their current situation. The trading of my-spouse-is-worse-than-your-spouse stories is something that is common, even in Christian circles, but it should be avoided at all costs. Never expose your spouse to ridicule by sharing their weaknesses and faults with others just to have the comfort of finding people who will sympathize with you. Great rewards await the person who will trust the Lord to bring someone who will invest himself or herself in the reconciliation and success of your marriage.

The same holds true when seeking advice and counsel regarding wayward or rebellious children. Swapping stories of your child's foolish actions may make you feel understood in that moment, but your family will be no closer to restoration when the conversation is over.

I promise you that when you spend time pouring out your concerns and worries to the Lord first, He will be faithful to place someone on your heart who will be able to speak life and hope into your situation. This someone will walk the journey with you in faith, always pointing you to the unfailing faithfulness of God.

Years ago, I walked through a two-year battle of having lumps in my breasts. My mother is a twenty-year breast cancer survivor, and I've had countless friends walk through this battle. My great aunt (on my mother's side) died from this horrible disease.

Getting that first phone call saying that they had found suspicious lumps in both sides sent me reeling! Immediately, the Lord placed two women on my heart, and I quickly called them. I received prayer and instantly felt immeasurably better. I then felt ready for the series of tests that awaited me.

I took a trusted friend with me for the first procedure. She shared my joy when most of the suspicious lumps were eliminated. But it didn't eliminate enough of them to narrow down the testing to just one side.

So back to the imaging center we went, this time for a sonogram. Bingo! This test showed that all had been eliminated except for one final lump. I was told that this one would require a biopsy. There was only one problem. I was leaving for a family vacation the next morning. I set the appointment for two weeks later, and my friend and I left the office. In the car, my friend shared that the Lord had given her a word concerning a specific strategy I was to follow while waiting for the biopsy.

While on vacation, I cried out to the Lord daily during my prayer time, followed the strategy that He laid forth, and somehow managed to create amazing memories in the process. When I returned home, I went in for the biopsy and received the report that we had been praying for: no cancer!

About nine months later, I found a lump in my right side. I referred to this situation in the last chapter. God gave me a vision of Him casting the lump into the sea. As I mentioned, the lump was never found again.

Several months after that—you guessed it—I had another suspicious scan result. I knew the drill by now. I also started to believe that the Lord was using me to break this curse of cancer off the generations that would come after me.

We are often unaware that words or decisions that took place generations before us, have left us open to reoccurring illnesses. We can see this in the patterns of fractured relationships as well.

Standing in faith on His Word and promises during this two-year battle severed the ties of breast cancer from not only my body but also the bloodlines that were still to come. Seeing His faithfulness over and over, added victories under my belt that no amount of medical reasoning is able to explain away.

During those two years, less than a handful of people knew what was going on. Why? As I said, this was a battle to remove the evil of breast cancer from generations to come. I could not afford to have anyone speak words of fear or doubt into the atmosphere around me. This was crucial. I could not entertain any what-ifs—none.

This may seem foolish to you. After all, what if? What if this was cancer? What if I did lose all my hair? (That's vain, I know) What if I did need years of treatment? What if I wasn't going to be healed this side of Heaven? What if?

I'm not saying that this should be the strategy for all situations; this isn't a blueprint. But I did clearly hear from the Lord, and I had to obey. Early on, I knew in my spirit that in that season and circumstance, I was not to entertain any thoughts other than the lumps being completely gone. Obeying the Holy Spirit meant not sharing this with anybody outside of a handful of people.

Speaking life is more than just the words that are coming out of *my* mouth. Words have power, whether they are words of faith or words of fear. When spoken with emotion and faith, they are even more powerful. Sharing my battle with someone who may have lost a loved one or had her own negative, fear-filled experience with breast cancer was an opportunity for another person to interject words of doubt into my miracle.

Even if I was completely confident in someone's love for me, I had to be 100 percent sure of that person's faith and belief in my *total* healing. I had to do everything in my power to make sure that any words that were spoken into the atmosphere concerning my situation agreed with Heaven's words.

Revelation 12:11 tells us that we overcome by "the blood of the Lamb and the word of our testimony." Our words, whether they are positive or negative, are our testimony to everyone who is watching.

The Importance of Worship

Another way to put the right words into the atmosphere and one thing that I can always count on to keep me focused on God's goodness is worship music. When I look through my playlists, I can see an intentional selection of songs for each season that I have walked through. Music is a very powerful tool for me. I love all types of music. I know that music can change my mood in an instant and in either direction. I am very susceptible to feelings of melancholy. When I am in a season of contending for a miracle, the right playlist can make all the difference.

Just like the selection of people that I bring into my confidence, the Holy Spirit is ever ready to highlight songs that will help me sing out in agreement with the things that I believe God for in any given circumstance. When I have a playlist created, I play it at every opportunity: while I'm driving, getting ready for the day, doing the dishes, or cooking dinner—whenever I can.

A song that is currently being sung by worship teams in churches across America right now is called "Champion." It is produced by Bethel Music[1] and sung by Dante Bowe. I've included the words to the bridge of this song. As you read them, ask yourself this question: How different would my life look if I truly believed the words of this song?

When I lift my voice and shout
Every wall comes crashing down

---

[1] written by Brandon Lake, Steffany Gretzinger, Dante Bowe, Jonathan Jay and Tony Brown

I have the authority

Jesus has given me

When I open up my mouth

Miracles start breaking out

I have the authority

Jesus has given me

The question is not, are your words powerful, but rather, will you open your mouth and declare with confidence your authority?

I'll close this chapter with a powerful reminder from the book of Hebrews. Hebrews 1:3 puts it all into perspective.

The Son is the dazzling radiance of God's splendor, the exact expression of God's true nature—his mirror image. He holds the universe together and expands it by the mighty power of his *spoken word*. He accomplished for us the complete cleansing of sins, and then took his seat on the highest throne at the right hand of the majestic One. (TPT, emphasis mine)

Wow! If His Word can accomplish all that, and if we are made in His image, and if we are told in scripture that we can accomplish even more than Jesus did, maybe we should be intentional in choosing words that bring life and advance His purposes!

Any time I sense that silence is causing fear and doubt to creep in, I put on my playlist and sing in agreement with God's promises. It is a great re-focuser and reminder: I am partnering with the all-powerful, already-victorious One.

3

Armor Up

He will cover you with his feathers. He will shelter
you with his wings. His faithful promises are your
armor and protection. (Psalm 91:4 NLT)

Whether we acknowledge it or not-we are in a battle!
It is a battle between death and life, indifference and
passion, and mediocrity and purpose. But the Lord
has not left us weak and defenseless. He has given us
everything that we need to not only fight the battle, but
to win. Even in our darkest valley, His shed blood has
guaranteed our victory. His provision is complete.

His Word instructs us, "Put on all of God's
armor so that you will be able to stand firm against all
strategies of the devil." (Ephesians 6:11 NLT). I love
the way that the Passion Translation phrases it: "Put on
God's complete set of armor provided for us, so that you

will be protected as you fight against the evil strategies of the accuser." Two things jump out at me from this scripture:

1. We are to engage in the fight.
2. We can walk protected against the evil strategies of the accuser.

If you are contending for a miracle, then it is safe to say that you are in a battle. And if you are in a battle, putting on your armor *every day* is crucial for your victory.

To find out just how thorough our Lord is in His provision for us, I looked up the word *armor* as it pertains to the armor of God. In the *Strong's Concordance*, the word for *armor* (in the Greek) is the word *panoplia*, which is actually a compound word made up of two Greek words. One is the word *pas*, meaning *every*, and the other is *hoplon*, meaning *weapon*. In the *Helps Word studies* reference, it is defined as, "A complete set of defensive and offensive armor, i.e. everything needed to wage successful warfare; the full resources the Lord gives to the believer so they can successfully wage spiritual warfare." Did you notice the word *successful*? How great is that?

Putting on the full armor of God has been a vital part of every miracle that has come to pass in my life. Specifying the armor pieces out loud helps me to remember that I am not in a battle against flesh and blood but against spiritual forces in the heavenly places (see Ephesians 6:12). This helps me to not waste time and energy fighting against my husband, my children, a doctor's diagnosis, a corrupt boss, pending financial disaster, or any of the other people and things of this world that are merely distractions.

There have also been times when the miracle that I was believing for required a victory for someone else. Praying the armor of God over that person (providing he or she was a believer or under my authority) has made a tangible and noticeable difference.

In this chapter, I want to take some time on each

piece of armor and share some scriptures and promises that coincide with them. This will help expand your understanding of the importance of each piece. I like to put on the armor of God from top to bottom. So let's start at the head.

The Helmet of Salvation

When I pray, I prefer to speak the words as they are written in the scriptures back to the Lord. I just feel an increased power and a higher level of confidence when I'm declaring what God has already spoken to be true. Sometimes I struggle with finding the words to express myself, and I can get caught up in questioning what I have the authority to claim. Declaring the words straight from the scriptures helps me stay focused.

When I started to put on the armor of God regularly, I needed it to feel relevant. So I would ask myself, *What does a helmet protect? What does my salvation have to do with it?* This is where the Lord led me.

The helmet protects the head. The head is synonymous with the mind, it is the place of knowledge, and it is where our thoughts reside. In battle, we need to have the mind of Christ, which the Word of God assures us that we have (see 1 Corinthians 2:16). It also says that we can have the same mind in us that is in Christ Jesus (see Philippians 2:5). Second Timothy assures us that we have been given a sound mind. Because we are commanded in 2 Corinthians 10:5 to take every thought captive, it must be possible through the blood of Jesus to do so. Our salvation gives us the confidence that what He has promised in Scripture will come to pass and that what we are commanded to do is actually possible to accomplish.

Putting on the helmet of salvation places heavenly armor over our thoughts and minds, as we do battle in the spiritual realm. Our salvation makes us one with Christ; therefore, we are partakers in all of His protection and blessing. We must know to whom we belong and the things that our salvation entitles us to. We put our helmet on first because what we think and believe about who we are and where our help comes from will determine how effective every other piece of armor is in the battle we are fighting for our miracles.

Breastplate of Righteousness

What does the breastplate protect? Well for starters, it protects the heart. Proverbs 4:23 tells us to guard our hearts above all else, for it determines the course of our lives. The Passion Translation paints a more vivid picture: "So above all, guard the affections of your heart, for they affect all that you are. Pay attention to the welfare of your innermost being for from there flows the wellspring of life." Wow! I love that: "Guard the affections of your heart."

The condition of our hearts matters. When he went to anoint one of Jesse's sons as the next King of Israel, the Lord told Samuel that man looks at the outward appearance but that God looks at the heart (see 1Samuel 16:7).

If we are to effectively guard the affections of our heart, we need to cover it with the breastplate of righteousness. Scripture assures us that we have the right to do this, not by our own righteousness but by the righteousness of Jesus. Isaiah 61:10 says,

> I am overwhelmed with joy in the Lord my God! For he has dressed me with the clothing of salvation and draped me in a robe of righteousness. I am like a bridegroom dressed for his wedding or a bride with her jewels.

Isaiah also tells us that our righteousness is from the Lord (see Isaiah 54:17 NLT). Romans 3:22 tells us, "It is God's righteousness made visible through the faithfulness of Jesus Christ. And now all who believe in Him receive that gift" (TPT). So we are clothed in righteousness through the shed blood of Jesus. We can place that breastplate on surely and securely.

A breastplate also covers our vital organs. When we are asking the Lord for a healing miracle, we can picture us placing the breastplate of righteousness over our systems and organs, which will protect them from the enemy's attack. I truly believe that this has great impact in the spirit world and that it stops many disastrous health issues before they even manifest in the physical world that we live in.

Last, the breastplate of righteousness covers our backs. God has our backs—the attacks we can't see coming. The Bible tells us that the Lord is our rear guard (see Isaiah 52:12). The breastplate has us covered. His righteousness gives us the boldness and confidence to put it on and secure it with the assurance that Christ's righteousness is our righteousness.

The Belt of Truth

The belt of truth goes around our waists so that the Truth, which is Jesus, surrounds us. In John 8:44, Jesus calls satan "a liar and the father of all lies" (NLT). He calls Himself "the way, the truth and the life" (John 14:6). When we put on the belt of truth, we not only put on a spiritual barrier against the liar, satan, but we also put on the protection of Truth itself—Jesus!

Another name that the Bible uses for satan is the "accuser of the brethren" (Revelation 12:10). I find it telling that Holy Spirit didn't stop with the title of "accuser," but He went on to specify that the devil specializes in accusing believers. We will talk more about the ways that he tries to fill our minds with accusing words against each other in the next chapter.

Right now, I want to point out that he works overtime trying to remind you of your failures and mistakes, in the hope that you will lose heart and quit believing for your miracle. He wants you distracted and discouraged, so he whispers (let's be honest, sometimes he shouts) lies day and night, hoping you will decide that victory will always be out of reach.

We have a weapon against this: the belt of truth around our waists. Not only is Jesus the Truth, but so is every promise in the Word of God, which we can use to stand against the onslaught of lies spoken by our enemy.

The Word tells us in James 4:7 that as we turn to God and resist the devil, the devil will flee from us. When we turn to God, we are better able to resist the devil.

The enemy only uses the weapons that work. It's been my experience that once a lie or tactic stops working, due to our continued resistance, the devil flees. He may go grab another weapon, but we now have experience on our side and wins under our belt, so we are quicker to resist, and he is quicker to flee.

Shoes of the Gospel of Peace

One day while praying the armor of God on myself, I was interrupted by a vision. It was a thought with an accompanying picture in my mind, which has stayed with me ever since.

As I was praying and getting to the part where I put on the shoes of the gospel of peace, I saw myself entering a grocery store. Every step I took left a visible mark of peace behind. As I walked through the store, I could see others entering it. They were suddenly being overtaken with a feeling of peace as they stepped where I had stepped. I realized that when I put on the full armor of God, I was doing more than just protecting myself. I was offering others an opportunity to encounter Jesus.

For years, I would have to work myself up in order to feel confident sharing the gospel with others—especially strangers. I would almost plan my defense before I even shared the good news because I expected an argument. No wonder I hesitated to share Jesus with anyone. But what I've discovered is that the more confidence I have in who God is and who He wants to be in my life, the more I see Him doing the impossible on my behalf. The more of His peace that I walk in, the easier it is to share the good news with those around me.

When I pray this part of the armor upon myself or a loved one, I always thank the Lord that "He keeps me in perfect peace because I trust in Him and keep my thoughts fixed upon Him" (Isaiah 23:3 NLT). It's such a good reminder that I have scriptural authority to walk in peace regardless of my situation. I don't have to be tossed to and fro. I don't have to be thrown upon the rocks of every storm that hits the world I live in.

As I write this, it is June of 2020. I cannot think of a season in my lifetime in which we have needed peace more than we do now. A virus has swept over the whole world, leaving fear and panic in its wake. It has almost completely shut down our entire country. It has affected, in some way, every single person. Wild discrepancies on diagnosis, prevention, and supposed precautions seem to change daily, leaving many wondering who to put their trust and hope in. Just as people seemed to find their footing and start to venture out again, cities all across our nation suddenly came under siege with riots and looting. This forced a military presence and curfews.

We, as believers, need to be clothed in the peace, hope, and confidence, which only the gospel can give. We're told that God's peace is not like the world's peace. It is not dependent on what we can see or discern with our senses. It's 100 percent reliable and always available. It's a peace that only God can give. Believe me; when you are clothed in it, people notice! There is no easier way to lead others into a discussion about God's goodness and the hope that comes from the gospel of Jesus Christ than to walk in a peace that sharply contrasts with the chaos that the world is walking in.

Shield of Faith

People say that you can't see faith, but I disagree. Faith has a look. I know this because my unsaved family and friends ask me how I can be so calm in the midst of terrible and trying circumstances. They may not be ready to accept the truth about Jesus, but they see something visibly different in me. What they see is faith.

Ephesians gives us a complete and descriptive picture of what our shield of faith is used for. It says, "In every battle, take faith as your wrap-around shield, for it is able to extinguish the blazing arrows coming at you from the Evil One" (6:16, TPT). I love that we have a wrap-around shield. I love that we have a weapon that extinguishes the blazing arrows that come at us from the evil one. A blazing arrow that is extinguished does no harm.

I picture it working something like this. Our shield is our faith. This faith is not in ourselves or our abilities but in Christ's finished work on the cross. We have faith because of the completeness of what Jesus did on our behalves. It is the solid rock that we stand on. That means that our shield is impenetrable because it is made from our faith in Him. When we hold it up, it shines in stark contrast to the smudged and murky arrows of the enemy's lies. It cannot fail because it is not made by human hands.

In the physical world that we live in, a shield blocks the sword thrusts of an enemy. It also stops an arrow or spear from penetrating our bodies. Our shield of faith does the same thing for us in the spiritual world. The beautiful thing is that we don't have to adjust our shields when the arrows come from a different direction.

Holding up the shield of faith, our wrap-around shield, protects us when we stand immovable in our faith in Jesus. Our faith grounds and sustains us.

Sword of the Spirit

And take the sword of the Spirit which is the word of God. (Ephesians 6:17 NLT)

Oh, how I love the Word! It is our sword. It cuts through and cuts down every scheme that the enemy throws our way. I talked a lot about the completeness of God's Word in the first chapter. I showed you how God's Word has a promise for every battle that you could possibly face. That was not by accident.

If the only offensive weapon that the Lord has given us is His Word, it stands to reason that there is a specific heavenly-crafted sword for every situation that we face. While constructing the sword is God's responsibility, learning to wield it effectively is ours. Fortunately, it's not all that complicated.

Let's say that I am being bombarded with anxious

thoughts. I will do an online search for *scriptures that combat anxiety*. Then, with the help of the Holy Spirit, I highlight any scriptures that speak to what I am feeling at that moment. Finally, I will take these scriptures and write them on cards to speak as a declaration every time those feelings try to rob me of my peace.

Remember that God's Word is truth all the time. I don't need to wonder if He wants me to have peace. I know He does! I use His words like a sword, cutting down the lies of the enemy. I swing my sword boldly and full of faith as I declare,

> I am anxious for nothing, but in everything by prayer and supplication, with thanksgiving, I make my request known to God; and the peace of God, which surpasses all understanding, will guard my heart and mind through Christ Jesus. (NKJV)

We can do this for every lie that the enemy throws at us. Do you have financial burdens? There's a sword for that. Are you going through a bumpy season in your marriage? Yup! There's a sword for that. Are your kids making choices that bring you to your knees? Trust me; there is a razor-sharp, divinely-crafted sword especially for that!

I want to wrap up this chapter about putting on our armor with Ephesians 6:11–18. I've written it in declaration form. I'm using the Passion Translation because I feel that it creates the imagery that most mirrors the spiritual battle of our current age. I hope it fires you up.

> I put on God's complete set of armor provided for me, so that I am protected as I fight against the evil strategies of the accuser! My hand-to-hand combat is not with human beings, but with the highest principalities and authorities operating in rebellion under the heavenly realms. For they are a powerful class of demon-gods and evil spirits that hold this dark world in bondage.

Because of this, I wear all the armor that God provides so I am protected as I confront the slanderer, for **I am destined for all things and will rise victorious.**

I put on truth as a belt to strengthen me to stand in triumph. I put on holiness as the protective armor that covers my heart. I stand on my feet alert, then I am always ready to share the blessings of peace.

In every battle, I take faith as my wrap-around shield, for it is able to extinguish the blazing arrows coming at me from the Evil One. I embrace the power of salvation's full deliverance, like a helmet to protect my thoughts from lies. And I take the mighty razor-sharp Spirit-sword of the spoken Word of God.

But let us who live in the light be clear headed, protected by the armor of faith and love, and wearing as our helmet the confidence of our salvation. (1Thessalonians 5:8 NLT).

4

Keep No Record

An offended friend is harder to win back than a fortified city. Arguments separate friends like a gate locked with bars. (Proverbs 18:19 NLT)

"If you want to birth the miraculous, you cannot afford to waste time getting offended. Offense stops you from carrying the promise to full term, and you never know what God plans to do with a situation that offends you at first." (Heidi Baker-Birthing the Miraclulous)

It has been my personal experience that holding onto an offense robs more people of their miracles than any other thing—even unbelief. This is a huge statement!

I'm so confident of this truth that I am going to share much of my personal battle with offense. I do this with the hope that you will not stop until you have mastered the habit of letting go of an offense before it has a chance to put down roots in the deep places of your heart. The battle is *very* real and personal to me.

Before Jesus, I was probably one of the most offensive people you would ever meet. I'm not being harsh, and I'm not exaggerating. I had horrible boundaries. I was seriously one of the most selfish people that I knew. I was extremely manipulative, and I lied so fluidly that I would sometimes even fool myself. After several years of friendship with me, if you had miraculously not yet been offended by me, then it is definitely safe to say that I would have been deeply offended by you. I was truly that easy to offend.

I'm not being hard on myself here. I was well aware of it at the time. Because I am so grateful for the love and grace of Jesus, I am not embarrassed to admit this to you. The glory that He gets by the enormity of my transformation is worth any discomfort I could experience by exposing my past to you.

I am so humbled to be able to share some of

the insights and truths that the Lord has shown me over the years. If you take them to heart and decide to be intentional in applying them, I promise you will experience a freedom to love people like never before. You will open a direct pathway for God to do incredible miracles for you and through you. But first, here is a truth that is of vital importance.

More than a Feeling

Offense may sound like a feeling, but it is really a spirit. I cannot stress this strongly enough! It is the servant of an enemy who wants you so broken that you will be unable to step into the life Christ died for you to have.

We already talked about the fact that we do not wrestle against flesh and blood; our enemy is never human. That said, the devil uses people—often the people who are closest to us—to bring disappointment and hurt. Whether we want to admit it or not, we too have been used by the enemy for the same purpose in some of our most meaningful relationships. The spirit of offense splits families, churches, organizations, and friendships every single day. You've probably experienced this devastating force- probably even more than once.

When we recognize that offense is a spirit instead of a feeling, it keeps the ball in our court. We don't need to be overwhelmed by an emotion that we feel powerless to control. While hurt, anger, and disappointment are valid feelings when we think someone has wronged us, saying, "No," when this spirit tries to bring destruction and division allows the Holy Spirit to rush in. He brings the kind of comfort and peace that only His presence can deliver. We receive fresh, heavenly perspective and wisdom straight from the Throne Room. This wisdom will give us the ability to extend a supernatural forgiveness to those around us.

We must make the choice to attack and defeat the spirit of offense as it tries to rob us of our most important connections. The enemy wants us to think that being offended gives us power: power to demand an apology, to vent, to get our way, and to hurt the one who hurt us first. This is one of satan's great lies. When we walk in offense, we don't *get* power- we *lose* power! We bind ourselves to a master who is never satisfied and never done.

In chapter 2, we talked about the importance of resisting the devil

> *We must make the choice to attack and defeat the spirit of offense as it tries to rob us of our most important connections.*

so that he will flee from us. When we have spent years allowing ourselves to be easily offended, we will need to be prepared for a battle, as we look to free ourselves from something that the enemy has been able to use with great efficiency in the past. In my case, it was a prolonged, intense battle. Maybe you can relate.

A Learned Reaction

If you're like me, you learned to take offense at a very young age. Maybe your family was riddled with splits and divisions as mine was. It's possible that bitterness was such a part of your day-to-day life growing up that it never occurred to you that it was not acceptable.

I had a pretty close family when I was little. Sunday dinners at Grandma's house with all the cousins were almost a weekly thing. We went to holiday BBQs, birthdays, anniversaries, and graduations (You get the picture). Extended family was the norm and not the exception.

Then the day came when a huge misunderstanding split the family right down the middle. A random prank call to my grandmother about my cousin scared her so much that she called my mom for assistance. Although my mom didn't know it, her mother was the victim of a group of kids calling random phone numbers on a Friday night. They got lucky using a name that matched that of her grandson. They said that he was seen doing things that he wasn't supposed to be doing (things that were very dangerous).

In a panic, she called my mother, who willingly stepped in to help. When my mother called to inform my aunt, it set off a chain of events that left our family splintered in ways that we never fully recovered from. Accusations and assumptions left deep wounds of hurt. People that I saw on a regular basis now shunned my mother. A whole section of my family became off limits. To this day, the situation still brings up strong words and feelings, if mentioned in the wrong company.

As a child, one doesn't usually question whether what is happening is normal or not. Early on, I learned to disconnect when someone wronged me.

Maybe you grew up where a catastrophic event left wounds that were allowed to fester into hatred and self-destruction.

I was molested at a very young age by someone I trusted. I was forced to see that person regularly until the day he died. People who were supposed to protect me failed at their charge because of their own wounds and brokenness at being unprotected.

When situations like this happen at such a young age, they can create a wide-open door for the spirit of offense to come in and set up house. This begins a long series of choices that form deeply rooted habits of coping, which eventually become fertile soil for self-destructive behaviors. These fool you into thinking that you're the one in control. Control is very important to a person who has been violated, at any age. Unfortunately, being in control is just an illusion. Taking offense becomes a way of life and survival. It keeps us from forming the kind of healthy relationships that bring healing. But it doesn't have to stay that way.

When we give our pain to Jesus, we set out on a lifelong learning process with multiple opportunities to grow and go to the next level in our quest to become someone who is unoffendable. When we become a person who refuses to keep a record of wrongs, it gives us real power.

I got fresh revelation on this a few years back. My pastor had given me an opportunity to serve on a team that was asked to plan and execute a women's retreat. I was thrilled and honored. I hadn't been at the church very long, and I had never done that kind of planning before. I was on a team with women who were quite experienced, and fortunately for me, they were also full of grace.

Blame: A Doorway to Offense

My official title was Facilities Director. As you probably guessed, I was in charge of finding and securing our facility. After touring several locations, we decided on the best one. I went to work negotiating our price, the number of rooms that we would need to block, cancelation dates, etc. It was all very exciting. The number of rooms that we needed amounted to about two whole floors when all was said and done. For convenience, the hotel reserved the first and second floor rooms for us.

Two weeks before the retreat, I learned that a high school football team, which was on their way to a state championship, had booked the entire third floor of rooms- the floor right above where our one hundred women would be sleeping. These women would be leaving their children at home to get away for a relaxing weekend with Jesus. Maybe I'm just stereotyping here, but the thought of twenty-five to fifty high school boys coming and going on the floor above us sounded like a complete disaster.

I was in a full-fledged panic! My instincts kicked in, and the first thing I thought to do was find someone to blame.

Whoa, did you read that? My first reaction was to find someone to blame.

Huh?

Even in the heat of the moment, this struck me as odd. I asked the Lord about it, and He showed me something about this reoccurring pattern in my life: I had become programmed to blame.

I needed someone to blame because I had learned early in life that if someone else was to blame for my current situation, I didn't have to deal with it. If it was someone else's fault, it wasn't my responsibility to fix it. I could pass the blame and move on to the next situation.

The problem was that I would eventually run out of people to blame. That was the case with the facility for the retreat. There was absolutely no one that I could blame to make the problem go away. I had to deal with it and find a workable solution. The Lord was giving me a chance to partner with and trust Him in the crisis. In the process, I was able to identify a destructive pattern in my life and learn to replace it with a more productive way of handling things.

I sent out a prayer request to those who had committed to pray specifically for our retreat. In the end, the football team ended up choosing a different hotel. Learning to trust the Lord with these unexpected challenges was a life-altering experience for me. I was able to see that what seemed like an obstacle was no surprise to the Lord. He already had a solution. I just needed to seek Him first.

Often, His solution results in a more favorable

outcome than what we had originally planned in the first place. God's plans are always better than our plans. He will often use our trials as an opportunity to pour out His blessings on us, if we will choose to run toward Him instead of away from our challenges. I never looked at opposition the same way again.

I share this story for two reasons. One, I'm sharing to point out that blame is very closely related to offense. When we blame others for what is going on in our lives, we focus on the problem instead of believing God for the solution. Placing blame blocks our ability to hear from Heaven and keeps us bound in unforgiveness.

The other reason that I share this story is to show that many of the ways we function in our relationships with people are the result of lies that we have agreed with for many years. We don't realize that we are actually hurting ourselves by allowing these lies to create patterns regarding the way that we relate to others during trying situations.

We need to the take time to assess our

relationships while seeking input from the Holy Spirit. Then we can allow Him to bring truth into those places of our hearts where we have come into agreement with a lie spoken to us by the spirit of offense. When we do this, true and lasting freedom is close at hand.

Jesus warns us in Matthew 6:14– 15, "And when you pray, make sure you

We cannot simultaneously believe God for a miracle and lay up offenses against others.

forgive the faults of others so that your Father in heaven will also forgive you. But if you withhold forgiveness from others, your Father withholds forgiveness from you." Jesus goes on to tell us in Matthew 7:1–2, "Refuse to be a critic full of bias toward others, and judgment will not be passed on you. For you'll be judged by the same standard that you've used to judge others. The measurement you use on them will be used on you" (TPT). We cannot simultaneously believe God for a miracle and lay up offenses against others.

The truth is that sometimes things just happen.

Accidents occur, and situations come up, which are part of life and not the fault of any one person. It's a huge opportunity to press into the Lord and seek His perspective. Placing blame may be the way that you cope with unexpected challenges, but it is not the way that leads to true freedom.

Keeping No Record for Others

As if resisting the desire to take up an offense committed against ourselves is not hard enough, few things will entice us to partner with the spirit of offense like perceiving a wrong, real or imagined, against our children. Parents beware!

In March of 2015, a huge nationwide women's conference was about to take place in our city. As a student at our church's ministry school, my oldest son was set to serve on the production team. My youngest son had been invited too. He was to sit with his friend, who was on the worship team. Since men rarely attend our women's conference, I was super excited that both of my boys would be there and get a download of what the Lord had planned for the weekend.

Right before worship was about to begin, I heard that the worship team had a last-minute change of plans. For legitimate, logistical reasons, they would be sitting together in the front row. Since my son was not on the worship team, this change of plans would leave him sitting by himself in the back of the room- or so I thought. If you're a mother (or even married to one), you know that this was an instant invitation for a wrestling match with offense to begin.

Worship started, and along with it came the loud and forceful voice of the accuser. Accusation after accusation regarding the unfairness of the situation played through my head so loud that it made the worship music sound like a mere whisper in comparison. Declarations of the intentional slight against my son drowned out all words of truth regarding the intentions of people that I had trusted completely just moments earlier. Being overly concerned for my son's heart left mine totally exposed to the lies and flaming arrows of the evil one.

There must have been a slight opening in my spirit because the Lord was able to reach into the last sliver of my logical reasoning and drop this thought into my mind: *Right now in this moment, you have the choice to pick up this offense and place it on your child's shoulders. Resist it!* What He was showing me was this: As a mother, I had the ability to take up an offense on behalf of my child and place the full weight of that offense on him. This could cause his spirit to be offended. And, here is the kicker: I could do this even if he (or she) was not currently bothered by it.

Through the grace of God, I was able to stop and see that my son was not the least bit bothered by the change in the schedule. He was happy where he was, and it didn't occur to him to feel offended. Do you remember the quote from Heidi Baker at the beginning of this chapter?

If you want to birth the miraculous, you cannot afford to waste time getting offended. Offense stops you from carrying the promise to full term, and you never know what God plans to do with a situation that offends you at first.

God set this whole situation up ahead of time. By refusing to take offense with the last-minute decisions of others, both my son and his friend were able to receive everything that the Lord had prepared for them because they were right where they needed to be at this amazing, life-changing conference.

This experience shed new light on the power (and loss) of taking up offenses on behalf of my children. It allowed me to press into worship for the remainder of the night. Worship was all the more powerful because I had won the battle against the spirit of offense only moments earlier. It was truly miraculous! I never could have had this revelation on my own. It caused me to be ever vigilant, from that day forward, to recognize the enemy's schemes regarding the spirit of offense and protecting the hearts of my children.

Children are generally hard to offend and quick to forgive. This makes them ill equipped to handle the multitude of offenses that are placed on them by their easily offended parents. By thinking that we are experts at judging the intentions of others, we open doors for the spirit of offense to come in and capture the thoughts and hearts of our children. I know that sounds harsh, but I'm saying this as someone who has been there. I know that the consequences are truly that important!

In hindsight, I can tell you that the individuals whom the enemy desperately wanted to separate me from that night were the same people that the Lord was about to use to bring comfort and support to our family on the following day. I didn't know it at the time, but in just a few short hours, tragedy would strike our household.

We were going to lose a beloved family pet suddenly, without warning, and due to the careless mistake of another. Those people who had made the decision to change where the worship team sat at the conference were the same ones whom God would call to come alongside us and embrace us in our time of need. In the middle of hosting a huge conference, they took the time to hold us, pray for us, and check in on us to make sure that we were okay. Their prayers and genuine concern for each of us helped us to stay present for the rest of the weekend.

My older son received the call to become a pastor at that same conference. How different it would have turned out if the destructive spirit of offense had been allowed to have its way, if I had ignored that still small voice the night before, and had instead run with the accusations swirling in my head. I would have left my family without the covering that God had so graciously provided.

Lifetime Consequences

On the back cover of his bestselling book, *The Bait of Satan*, John Bevere says that our response to offense will determine our future. I couldn't agree more. The testimony I just shared with you is just one example of many that proves it. I have countless more! There have been numerous times when the spirit of offense has rushed in forcefully against someone in my life, who, unbeknownst to me, was the very person that I would need in the hours and days to come.

If you are bombarded with accusing thoughts against someone, this should set off a loud warning signal that causes you to stop and pray immediately. Chances are that you are being set up. The very person who holds the key to a victory in your life is about to become the target of your enemy. The enemy wants to bring offense between the two of you, rendering the other person powerless to give you aid. Satan knows that this person is critical to you in this moment, and he is working overtime to drive a wedge of offense in your heart so that you will be separated from that individual.

Do not be fooled! Your enemy has been defeated, but he is not stupid. This attack is not random, and your offense will feel quite justified. It may even have a seed of truth and real hurt mixed in for good measure. Stand strong, drop to your knees, and cry out to God to give you heavenly perspective. Journal, if necessary, to get your feelings out. Then wait upon the Lord to give you strategy and direction. I promise, time with the Lord will take the sting out of the offense and allow you to proceed with wisdom.

When I am being assailed by accusing thoughts against someone important in my life, I go into my prayer closet and cry out until I get peace. Often, I have to write out all of my angry words and justifications against that person until I am spent. Then peace can enter in. I find that it is always better than letting the emotions carry me away to actions, which I will regret later on. There are times that I've had to do this night after night for a season.

Am I saying that there is never a time to confront? No, absolutely not! We will discuss some scriptures about confrontation in just a moment. But it is never the right time to confront someone when the emotions of hurt and anger are still coursing through your veins. If you are too emotional to sleep, trust me, you are too emotional to confront someone in a way that is productive and honoring.

This is so important to the Lord that He will give us multiple opportunities to choose to become free from offense. He will often provide several chances to overcome the power of offense so that we can walk freely and wholly, love deeply, and forgive quickly. Sometimes when we are going through trials that are meant to free us, it can feel like everyone that we trust has suddenly turned against us. Does this sound familiar?

Jesus experienced the same things on His journey to the cross as, one by one, His closest friends betrayed, denied, and left Him to die alone. But (here's the really good news) He has forever and completely conquered the spirit of offense and permanently secured our victory, if we will only choose to follow in His footsteps.

When Confrontation Is Needed

Jesus gives us the formula for confrontation in the book of Matthew.

> If another believer sins against you, go privately and point out the offense. If the other person listens and confesses it, you have won that person back. (Matthew 18:15 NLT)

Here's the key. Don't miss it. It says, "If another believer sins against you." First, you must determine and be absolutely certain that the other person has sinned. If there is no sin, there is no biblical basis for your confrontation.

If we're being honest, more often than not, we

get hurt and offended because the people in our lives act and respond in ways that are different than the way that we think they should. We take it personally when someone makes a decision that we deem is unfair or unjust. Thinking we have all the pieces, we predetermine their motives and make a judgment as to their intentions. This is why it is imperative that we spend time seeking the Lord. He, and only He, has all the pieces and knows the hearts and intentions of those involved.

We've been given a strategy. Proverbs 17:9 says, "Love prospers when a fault is forgiven, but dwelling on it separates close friends" (NLT). I have lost count of the times that offense has tried to divide me from the very people that the Lord has put in my life to benefit me with blessing and spiritual growth. I get extremely emotional and overwhelmingly grateful when I meditate on how the Lord has taught me to recognize quickly when this spirit is trying to separate me from my lifeline here on earth. It takes obedience and discipline to wait upon the Lord instead of reacting to the destructive emotions raging wildly in my head. It's hard, it takes time and practice, but it is worth it.

Keeping No Record against Our Spouses

Marriage can sometimes feel like a daily battle against the spirit of offense. By far, the people who are able to hurt us the most are the people who are closest to our hearts. Who is closer to us than our spouses?

In an effort to be transparent, I will admit that this area is where I have the biggest need for growth and victory. This is not because my spouse is particularly difficult or offensive, but because there is nothing more powerful to display the miraculous that plays out in my life on a regular basis than a strong, loving, and offense-free marriage.

The relationship between Christ and the Church is compared several times in scripture to the relationship of a husband and his bride (see Ephesians 5:25–27, John 3:29, and Revelation 21:2). Is it any wonder that satan has launched his most constant, violent, and forceful attacks against marriages, especially Christian marriages? No matter what the state of your marriage is in right now, I am convinced that it can be transformed into a relationship that provides safety and security for both parties.

I will make no promises except one. Choose to take every offense against your spouse to the Lord first, wait for His instruction (either through His Word, the Holy Spirit's prompting, or the trusted, prayerful counsel of a spiritual mentor), and do exactly what He instructs you to do. Then you will be able to walk in a peace and confidence that will keep you moving toward the miracles of God for your life. If you are believing God for a miracle, I can almost guarantee that you will need to refuse to keep a running tab on the wrongs committed against you.

I will leave you with some words from what is commonly referred to as the love chapter.

Love is patient and kind. Love is not jealous or boastful or proud or rude. It does not demand its own way. It is not irritable, and it keeps no record of being wronged. It does not rejoice about injustice but rejoices whenever the truth wins out. Love never gives up, never loses faith, is always hopeful, and endures through every circumstance. (1 Corinthians 13:4–7 NLT)

This should be our goal in every relationship. It is impossible in our own strength, but with the help of the Holy Spirit, we truly can walk out from under the spirit of offense and leave ourselves open so that we can see the miraculous play out in our relationships and lives.

5

Hold Fast

Let us hold tightly without wavering to the hope we
affirm, for God can be trusted to keep His promise.
(Hebrews 10:23 NLT)

While you are waiting for a miracle, I can almost
guarantee that there will come a time when you will
need to hold fast. It may be for a period of days or it
may take several years, but it will undoubtedly be part
of your journey. If you're not careful, you will miss
one of the greatest opportunities that you, as a follower
of Jesus, have the chance to partner with Heaven and
experience the deeper things of God.

After the Thrill

Once the need for a miracle has been identified in my life,
there is almost an excitement as I search the scriptures
and see what God has to say about it. Declaring the

Word of God in faith, praising Him in worship, and receiving encouraging words from my trusted friends and mentors are all part of the exhilarating process of walking hand in hand with Jesus and being reminded of His great love for me.

But after the freshness of the newly given promises has worn off, the valley comes. The enemy starts to whisper his favorite question, *Did God really say...?* In this place, uncertainty can start to creep in. Sometimes, when I'm focused and taking care to get the rest and refreshment that I need with the Lord, the door is only open a crack before I slam it shut. At other times, I am busy and involved in self-pursuits. Then the door is flung wide open, and doubts come storming in like an army. In these times, holding fast becomes work. It can feel lonely and hopeless. It can also feel like I will never see the promises come to pass.

Hope in the Waiting

As I write, I am walking this out in real time. I am waiting. Some days I am full of faith, and some days-not so much. When the company my husband worked for last year announced that his division was being eliminated, we were given several months advance notice. It never occurred to us that he would not move from his then current job into another job immediately. When we shared what was going on with our friends and prayer partners, they received several words of promise from the Lord, which they quickly shared with us. We were so encouraged! Then things didn't happen as quickly as we had hoped they would.

We could never have predicted that more than four months would pass before an offer of employment would come forth. Even then, the offer fell far short of what we were believing God for and what we believed that He had promised us through the prophetic words that we had received. Though the delay was not what we expected, our belief in who God is and what He said remains unchanged. He is a God who keeps His promises, and we both continue to hold fast to the promises that He has given us. We are holding fast for our miracle.

I'm grateful that my husband was given a job that would allow him to remain employed and work from home when our country shut down due to the COVID-19 virus. I am grateful that all of our bills are paid, and we always have food on the table. I'm thankful for all of God's provision while at the same time, I am believing that every promise we've received will be fulfilled. Yes, I believe, but it's not always easy. There have been (and will continue to be) days when fear tries to rob me of my faith and keep me from continuing to do the things that He has daily set before me to accomplish.

Some of my most treasured times with the Lord have come in this phase of the journey—when what stands in front of me is the opposite of what I have been promised. This is *not* the time to give up. It's not the time to quit. It's always too soon to stop believing. It's here that I feel God's love for me the most because it is here that I need Him the most. The place where your circumstances defy your miracle is the place where you will find God waiting and ready to remind you of who He is and how much He loves you.

A few months back, I saw a post on social media that was so perfectly timed to what I was going through that I stopped and quickly repented of my doubt and unbelief. It said this:

Don't let what you see make you forget about what I (God) said.

So often, what lies in front of us can cause us to doubt what God has declared as truth. Sometimes, what used to inspire us is drowned out by the steady, persistent hum of unbelief, which is shouted repeatedly to us by a distrusting world that lives in fear and skepticism.

It's Always Too Soon to Stop Believing God

Hold fast! Speak the promises that God has given you boldly. Worship Him with all you are. Call a friend, reach out for prayer, and do whatever you need to do, but do not turn away from the belief that God is good and that He has good things in store for you. Weeping may indeed last for the night (or the week or the year), but joy does come in the morning. Psalm 30:5 assures us that this is so.

The Lord has never—and I mean *never*—failed to bring me comfort in my time of need. The nights of crying out to the Lord and wondering when His promises will come to pass have been my greatest times of growth. It's here in the fire that I become purified and made strong. Afterward, I can boldly declare Psalm 40:1–2, which says,

> I waited patiently for the Lord to help me, and he turned to me and heard my cry. He lifted me out of the pit of despair, out of the mud and the mire. He

set my feet on solid ground and steadied me as I walked along. He has given me a new song to sing, a hymn of praise to our God. Many will see what he has done and be amazed. They will put their trust in the Lord.

Is there any greater testimony than that of our victory being the reason that someone else puts his or her trust in the Lord?

The truth is that at some point while waiting for your miracle, you will face what seems like overwhelming evidence that God will not come through. It will appear as though you must have heard wrong. Don't you believe it! Luke 12:2–3 gives us the assurance that we need to stand strong in the storm of worry and fear.

The time is coming when everything that is covered up will be revealed, and all that is secret will be made known to all. Whatever you have said in the dark will be heard in the light, and what you have whispered behind closed doors will be shouted from the housetops for all to hear.

The times of crying out in the darkness and declaring His truth behind the door of your secret place will bring forth a harvest. It will be so full that there will be blessing enough, not only for you but also for those who have been watching and waiting to see if God can be relied on to keep His Word.

Over the years, I have had to make the choice to hold fast several times as I waited for the final victory to unfold. I've also had the great privilege of joining others on the battlefield of prayer as they have contended for their miracle.

It's Not a Question of If but of When

One such battle is that of a friend whose unwavering faith has been a constant inspiration to me as I've struggled in the seasons between receiving the promise and walking in the fulfillment of it. The following is a glimpse into the steps that she has taken to trust God in the waiting. I am sharing it with her permission. She writes,

> I have seen God do many miracles. Miracles in the lives of others and my own life personally. I have seen Him heal suddenly and also over a period of time. I have experienced sudden relief from symptoms in my body and have also stood on promises from God and waited for healing to come. The question for me, I discovered, was not, "does God heal?" but "will He?"
>
> In one particular season of my life, after battling symptoms with my gut for years, I had become frustrated. In my teenage years, my parents had taken me to specialists and many doctors to no avail. When I began going to a great church, I learned how to seek the Lord for answers and remedy. With this new revelation, I had times of victory, but then another setback would come. I sought the Lord, I received prayer: and when I say "received prayer" I don't mean I asked somebody once—I had

people pray for me hundreds of times, and that is no exaggeration. I knew that God promised healing to me and I believed Him. I felt like I had done all I could do, and I was frustrated.

After a particularly rough few days that resulted in my being in bed, I told my husband, "That's it! We're seeing the holistic nutritionist!"

My husband, knowing that I love the Lord and knowing how I have suffered with symptoms, gently said, "I will do whatever you want. We can absolutely see her. I just want to make sure that when we do, we're not making this decision because we're mad."

I didn't like his answer. Not at all. But of course he was right! I couldn't just make a decision in haste because I was angry with the Lord and what seemed to be a lack of results. I couldn't force God's hand and, while upset, make a choice without His blessing. I was reminded immediately of the story of Ishmael. In Abraham's desperation to bring about a promise from God, He compromised and attempted to make something happen on his own.

I did not want to sacrifice the promise God had given me and exchange everything for my own way or my own expectations. I then began to ask God to change my heart. I didn't want to be mad. I didn't want to be frustrated. I wanted to see things the way He did.

Several weeks after asking the Lord to change my heart, He did! It came suddenly and unexpectedly and brought such freedom.

I had been listening to audio Scriptures on repeat, and one particular verse just stuck with me. Every time I heard it, I found myself weeping and overcome by the goodness of God towards me.

"Then I saw a new heaven and a new earth, for the old heaven and the old earth had disappeared. And the sea was also gone. And I saw the holy city, the new Jerusalem, coming down from God out of heaven like a bride beautifully dressed for her husband. I heard a loud shout from the throne, saying, 'Look, God's home is now among his people! He will live with them, and they will be his people. God himself will be with them. He will wipe every tear from their eyes, and there will be no more death or sorrow or crying or pain. All these things are gone forever.' And the One sitting on the throne said, 'Look, I am making everything new!' And then he said to me, 'Write this down, for what I tell you is trustworthy and true.' And he also said, 'It is finished! I am the Alpha and the Omega—the Beginning and the End. To all who are thirsty I will give freely from the springs of the water of life. All who are victorious will inherit all these blessings, and I will be their God, and they will be my children.'" (Revelation 21:1–7 NLT)

It was like my eyes were being opened and a fog was clearing away. I realized the question is never "if the Lord will keep His promise to me," but more of an understanding of when.

Every promise WILL be fulfilled. As a believer in Jesus Christ, eternity is promised to me, and, with the promise of eternity, no more death or sorrow or crying or pain. This is for sure. I never ever have to question this. Eternity, where everything is new, belongs to me.

Healing therefore belongs to me and is already a surety. I can now confidently say "I am healed!" because whether I see it right this minute, or experience it forever in eternity, I have it. I don't have to wonder if the Lord will keep His promise. He already has. The issue at hand isn't a matter of God coming through or His faithfulness to me. He has come through and He is forever faithful. The issue is in my expectation of timing. All of sudden, the stress and the burden of wondering "if" I would be healed was completely removed from me and I was free to just believe God! I knew in my heart that God had brought great freedom. I still feel it even as I write; the joy in knowing what is promised to me.

I released my expectations to the Lord and told Him, "You have healed me. Whether it is this side of eternity or not, you have done it. While I am on this earth, I will continue to believe You and will do whatever you want me to do and steward my body in a way that allows it to function the way You need it to while I'm here."

Shortly after this revelation, I felt like it was time to begin seeing the holistic nutritionist. While there has been progress in my body and a closeness from the Lord in the process, I am still most in awe of the change in my heart. I have changed my diet and my lifestyle and yet, the shift in my perspective and expectation has brought even greater healing to me. There is a depth of believing God and trusting Him more than before. There is a confidence in the goodness of God and His promises. I am so very grateful.

If you are in a season of waiting, may the Lord do for you what He did for me. May the truth of His faithfulness and kindness settle on your heart and may you delight in the promise of eternity. May He shift your expectations and give you His perfect perspective. He's just that good!

I love when she says, "Whether I see it right this minute, or experience it forever in eternity, I have it." What an incredible perspective! May this increase your faith and bring you into a place of peaceful reassurance as you continue to move forward in the confidence that He will fulfill every promise He has made to you.

You Can't Rush God

Please, do not take her reference to the story of Ishmael lightly. Sarah tried to manipulate the timing of when God's promise to give her a child would come to pass. As Abraham's wife, Sarah would have had the legal authority to claim any child of Abraham's who was conceived by her servant. Even so, the child of a servant was a poor substitute for the promised child of her womb (no matter what the law said). Her momentary refusal to hold fast to the promise of God came with disastrous consequences.

There will be times when the temptation to substitute a lesser version of the promise— one that we can produce immediately—will come.

> *Don't settle for something crafted with human hands when you can have something fashioned in the workroom of Heaven.*

But it will do so at the expense of the perfect fulfillment of God's miraculous provision. The chance for Him to get the glory will be wasted. Things will most often look completely hopeless just moments before your breakthrough, so don't settle for something crafted with human hands when you can have something fashioned in the workroom of Heaven.

An Example Worth Following

Let us choose instead to be like the women who held fast to Jesus (see Mark 5). Scripture tells us that this woman's affliction was a continual flow of blood, which caused her great suffering. (see verse 25) It went on for twelve years! This wasn't a minor inconvenience. She spent everything that she had going from doctor to doctor, but she ended up worse than before (see verse 26). In those days, Jewish law would have required her to lose all connection with her community because of her condition. Yet she had the faith to risk unimaginable consequences, which would occur if she was caught out in public. She did this all in the hope that she would be able to touch the hem of Jesus's garment and be healed. She held fast.

While this is a great example of holding fast, another person's story begins just three verses before it in Mark 5:22. It's the story of Jairus. In scripture, we read that Jairus, who was the leader of the local synagogue, arrived just as Jesus showed up in the village. We're told that Jairus fell at His (Jesus's) feet and pleaded fervently with Him to come and heal his daughter, who was dying. Jesus agrees. While they are on the way to Jairus's house, the woman that we just read about got her miracle. Jesus could not resist her display of unwavering faith. Although she was healed without a word from Him, Jesus had to stop and talk with her. During what appears to be an untimely delay, messengers from Jairus's village came to tell Jairus that his daughter had died. Jesus, who overheard what was said, remained undeterred. He told the desperate father, "Don't be afraid. Just have faith." Let us pick up the story in verse 37.

Then Jesus stopped the crowd and wouldn't let anyone go with him except Peter, James, and John (the brother of James). When they came to the home of the synagogue leader, Jesus saw much commotion and weeping and wailing. He went inside and asked, "Why all this commotion and weeping? The child isn't dead; she's only asleep." The crowd laughed at Him. But He made them all leave, and He took the girl's father and mother and His three disciples into the room where the girl was lying. Holding her hand, He said to her, "Talitha koum," which means

"Little girl, get up." And the girl, who was twelve years old, immediately stood up and walked around. (Mark 5:37–42, NLT)

Jairus got his miracle. His daughter did indeed live. He too held fast and got his reward. We can see another principle that we've discussed previously at work here as well. We must be very careful whom we allow to speak into our miracle. Jesus knew the unbelief of the crowd. We're told that He made them all leave before He went into Jairus's house to heal his daughter.

The other thing that struck me is the opportunity Jairus would have had to be offended. After all, Jesus was on His way to Jairus's house when He was interrupted by this woman's persistence. I wonder if it was hard to stand against the temptation to blame this woman for his daughter's death. It's something worth considering.

Of course, our best example comes from Jesus. The Scripture tells us that we should keep our eyes on Jesus, the champion who initiates and perfects our faith.

Because of the joy awaiting him, he endured the cross, disregarding its shame (and excruciating pain). Now he is seated in the place of honor beside God's throne. (Hebrews 12:2 NLT, parenthesis mine)

Jesus had the promise that we would be restored back into fellowship with the Father through His sacrifice on the cross. It would guarantee our eternity with Him in Heaven.

But knowing the promise didn't mean it would be easy. Anyone who has ever studied Roman crucifixion knows how horrific it would have been. Jesus would have understood, ahead of time, what awaited Him on His journey to the cross. He knew what He would have to endure. Yet because of the promise, He chose to persevere.

I've mentioned this before, but it bears repeating. He was betrayed, denied, and abandoned by almost all of those whom He had faithfully and without reservation poured Himself into for years. He was mocked and scorned by the very ones whom He came to save. Yet through all of it, He held fast to the promise.

While you will most likely never be called on to experience trials this fierce, you will undoubtedly be given opportunities to take your faith to the next level. It may require more trust than you think you have. Press in anyway. He who promised is faithful. There is no doubt that choosing to hold fast brings a great reward. Make the decision to not let what you see distract you from what He said.

6

One More Thing

I am bruised and broken, overwhelmed by it all;
breathe life into me again by your living word. Lord,
receive my grateful thanks and teach me more of
how to please you. Even though my life hangs in the
balance, I'll keep following what you've taught me,
no matter what. (Psalm 119:107–109 NLT)

As I spent time with the Lord reflecting on the many
miracles that have played out in my life, He began to
highlight some consistencies. I saw five principles that
were markers on each journey from tragedy to triumph.
We've discussed each of these in depth in the last five
chapters of this book.

Yet there seemed to be more than just praying
truth. More than just speaking life, putting on the armor
of God, letting go of offenses, and choosing to hold fast
when everything looked hopeless and lost. While all of

those things were necessary elements in my being able to step into the miraculous with God, there is something more; a piece that is different every time.

Consistently Inconsistent

While our Father in Heaven has a love for us that is unfathomable and truly wants to pour out favor and blessing upon our lives and situations, I believe there is something that He desires even more: relationship. God is all about relationship! I know that you've heard me say this before. Still, we cannot lose sight of this very important critical fact while we are learning how to partner with Him to see the miraculous unfold in our lives.

So what is this sixth principle? What other element is needed so that we can see His plans and purposes unfold in our lives in ways that will leave us in a constant state of awe and wonder?

I don't know. Or rather, I don't know what it will be for you.

The Linchpin

Before you toss this book across the room in frustration, let me explain. This sixth step has been different every time for me. Don't let the fact that you can't identify it instantly fool you. This isn't a throwaway item. In many cases, it is a linchpin.

A linchpin is defined as "a fastener used to prevent a wheel or other part from sliding off the axle upon which it is riding." That is exactly what this sixth piece of our miracle puzzle is. Why? Because it is in this place where we *must* hear from God. It is in spending time seeking His face that we hear the specific battle strategy for the war that we are currently in. It's what keeps us connected to and in constant contact with our loving Heavenly Father.

Do you remember when I shared my story about needing to schedule a biopsy the day before we were due to leave on a family vacation? I mentioned that my friend who was with me received a word from the Lord as to the strategy that I was to take while we were on vacation and I waited for the biopsy and its results. The Lord wanted me to anoint daily, the area where the lump was found with frankincense oil and to declare that the lump had completely dissolved. This, of course, was in addition to the other things I was already doing. These instructions were directly from the Throne Room and for that specific situation.

A different strategy came for each lump that would come in the two years that followed. It was as though each time, I received a personal confirmation from the Lord that He was in the battle with me. It was His way of inviting me into a deeper more personal relationship with Him, where I sought His face, and He answered me. Jeremiah 33:3 tells us, "Call to me and I will answer you, and will tell you great and hidden things that you have not known" (NLT).

We need this all-important linchpin to keep us *fastened* to God. Without it, we run the risk of thinking that we can just follow a formula to get what we want to from God. Without this relational element where we hear personally from the Lord, we are left with just a list of steps. We will quickly fall into a pattern of trying to earn a miracle from God, or worse, we will start to believe that we can manipulate God into giving us a miracle.

The Crucial Element

There is always the risk when writing a book that gives a set of action items or principles that the reader will end up just going through the motions and then wind up disillusioned with God when the actions don't produce the desired result. This is one of the reasons why I put off writing this book. Still, I couldn't ignore that the other things that I was doing were bringing such freedom and breakthrough in my life.

After sitting with the Lord, I realized that there was always one critical step. In many cases, this was actually two or three steps that were different in each circumstance. It was here that I spent time sitting before the Lord. It was here that my faith was tested and the need to hear from Him became what kept me close to Him and at His feet. It is what prevented me from doing things in my own strength.

For example, when I needed a miracle for my child, the Lord had me pray directly in his room. These were such sweet times of feeling the presence of the Holy Spirit invade my child's room as I spoke and prayed the promises of God over his life.

Another time while believing for a great financial breakthrough in my marriage, the Lord had me make our bed, pray over it, and anoint it every day. That may sound ordinary to you, but I was not a huge make-the-bed-every-day kind of person. The unexpected blessing that I found during this season was that it really ministered to my husband. Unbeknownst to me, he loves a freshly made bed. Who knew? God knew! We must never lose sight of the fact that God is all-knowing. He knows the things that we do not know.

I'm reminded of a great miracle that happened earlier this year. Actually, God was setting this up well before then. My father was suffering with Alzheimer's disease. Even though he was still able to remember us, his mind and body were rapidly deteriorating. We decided to purchase airline tickets to take the family for one last trip to see him.

Taking a family of five to Chicago is not a cheap endeavor, so we decided that it would be combined with some fun family activities and given as a Christmas present. Unfortunately, my father passed away in the beginning of November. We decided to take the trip anyway, but we had several schedules to juggle.

In the end, I chose to go to Chicago four days before the others to have some one-on-one time with my mother and each of my siblings. My brother was staying with my mom to help her and I was especially excited to get some extra time with him, as we have lived on opposite sides of the country for close to two decades.

When I arrived and he picked me up from the airport, I noticed that he was coughing pretty severely. He said that he'd had a cold that he'd been trying to shake for a few days. Upon entering my mom's house, I found my mother in the midst of a full-blown coughing fit. I thought, *Not good.* Still, I was so excited about catching up that I didn't give it much more thought.

That night, I was awakened in the middle of the night by coughing coming from both of their rooms; my room was directly in the middle of theirs. A wave of fear crashed down upon me. I began to worry that I was going to be sick by the time my family arrived, and our vacation would be ruined. I even started to think that it would be better for them to go on to the accommodations that we were renting without me so that I didn't infect them too.

In His mercy, the Lord completely derailed my train of thought. After declaring my go-to scriptures for peace (see Philippians 4:6–7 and Isaiah 26:3), I began to see things in a more heavenly light. I started by taking up my authority and sent fear to the cross. Then Jesus laid out the strategy that I was to follow so that I could walk in victory over any illness that was trying to come on me.

First, I was to anoint both doors into my bedroom with oil and declare my freedom from sickness and disease because of the shed blood of Jesus. Next, I was to take communion every single day that I was there. Finally, I was to play a specific song on repeat the whole night while I slept.

Now, here's the first miraculous part: I have *never* been able to get deep rest when music or any other voices are playing in the background. This time, however, I slept sound and restful the whole night and every night after that.

One night, the enemy tried to wake me up with symptoms of a sore throat. I sent the symptoms to the cross and declared the truth that Jesus bore all of my sickness at the cross (see Isaiah 53:4 and Matthew 8:17). Another time, one of my family members said that they heard me coughing all night. I refused to agree with that statement (I didn't recall coughing even once). One afternoon, my mother became so ill that I took her to see the doctor. She was too light-headed to drive herself. Afterward, I put her straight in bed to get some rest.

Amazingly through this whole time and aside from the initial wave of fear, I had absolutely no battle with anxiety. The Lord had spoken, and I could feel His presence in every moment.

I share all of this with you because there was no earthly reason why I should have remained healthy. It was winter, so all doors and windows were closed, trapping stale, germ-riddled air inside. The room where I slept was between the two bedrooms where there was sickness. I had constant contact with both of my family members the whole time I was there.

I knew how to pray truth and speak life. I put my armor on every day. I held fast in the midst of discouraging circumstances. Even though I was easily able to resist placing blame on anyone, I am fully convinced that I would have succumbed to the sickness in the house had it not been for this specific strategy from the Lord. Not only did it keep me in perfect health, but it kept me in His perfect peace. I'll say it again. Relationship is so important to God!

Obedience Brings Blessing

This process of hearing from and receiving strategy from the Lord is a further affirmation of His great and far-reaching love for me. This does not mean, however, that following it is easy. Often, this step can be the hardest. As I spent time contemplating this, I believe that I saw a couple reasons why this is so.

First off, many times, what I am sure that I heard the Lord tell me to do doesn't make any sense. I mean, how could a specific song keep sickness away, especially when the song isn't "victorious" in nature? In the case of my time in Chicago, it was just a simple fifteen-minute spontaneous worship song. How can the simple act of making the bed and praying over it bring breakthrough in our finances? I know that the Word of God has power wherever it is spoken, so why do I need to physically be in my child's room declaring scripture? Wouldn't it have the same power if prayed from the privacy of my prayer closet?

While I have no specific answer to these questions, I do know that my obedience opened a door for the miraculous to enter in. We are given a clue in 1 Samuel 15:22. It says, "What is more pleasing to the Lord: your burnt offerings and sacrifices or your obedience to his voice? Listen! Obedience is better than sacrifice, and submission is better than offering the fat of rams" (NLT).

Think about it. Do you feel closer to your own child when he or she chooses to obey? Compare it to the connection that you feel when he or she chooses to ignore your instruction. Your child's obedience doesn't change the amount of love you have for him or her, but it does invite a closeness that rebellion does not. I'm not implying that the Lord is easily swayed by human feelings and emotions (as in He is not swayed by them to the degree that we are). He does, however, long for meaningful connection with us. Our obedience is like a sweet fragrance that He cannot resist being drawn to.

We're Not Alone

While searching for examples in scripture, I found that the things I've been asked to do so that I can experience the miraculous move of God are nothing compared to what others were required to do. Take Joshua and the Israelites, for example. They marched around the city of Jericho for seven days. The first six of those days, they walked quietly around one time.

On the seventh day, they marched around seven times. Then the ram's horn was blown, and the people gave a great shout. The walls fell down, and the city was conquered (see Joshua 6:1–7). The Lord could have brought about the destruction of the city and handed the Israelites this miraculous victory in many ways that would have made far better sense to me when reading about them thousands of years later. But it was obedience and not sense that the Lord was after.

Take Naaman. He was told to go and dip in the Jordan River seven times in order to be cleansed of leprosy (You can read about it in 2 Kings 5:1–14). Naaman, sulking in offense, pointed out that there were nicer, cleaner, and more refreshing rivers in Damascus, where he was from. It was just not logical. It may not have been logical, but it must have been necessary because Naaman went on (in verse 17) to declare his allegiance to the God of Israel. These stories seem to always point back to relationship.

Jesus used some pretty unorthodox methods to bring the Kingdom of Heaven here to earth while performing the many miracles recorded for us in the Gospels. Being led by the Holy Spirit, Jesus put His fingers in a man's ears so that the man could receive hearing. He made mud by mixing dirt with His spit and put it on one man's eyes so that the man could receive his sight. He sent ten lepers off to see the priests so that they would be healed while on their way. Jesus purposely waited until Lazarus was dead for four days before raising him from death to life. Surely, there were easier, more conventional, and more socially acceptable ways to perform the miracles that He did.

It's Worth the Struggle

The other five steps that I have mentioned in this book will not bring results without the *power* of God, but it can be applied without the *input* of God. A few of them can even bring results when applied by those who do not acknowledge Jesus as their Lord and Savior.

I know several people who have practiced the principle of speaking positive words and fully understand that holding onto offense is like a crippling poison. They are great about having a constant positive outlook, and in many ways, their lives look blessed. Some may even say that they live miraculously free of struggle and hardship.

But, living a life that seems miraculously free of strife is not the same as living a life where we see the miraculous move of a loving God and Father on behalf of the children He is irresistibly drawn to. Knowing the situation-specific will of God requires connection; it requires relationship.

Another reason why this sixth step has been hard for me is that oftentimes, it requires me to do something repeatedly. This is the place where the battle between obedience and obligation rages strongly. I have frequently found myself questioning the necessity of doing something over and over. I never want to give place to legalism, which is man's system of rules and regulations, which leads to bondage.

At the same time, I desire to be obedient to what God is instructing me to do. That's where the fight lies. It's the same *did God really say* struggle from the garden. This is also where the spirit of fear can find an opening. For example, when I was directed to listen to a specific song on repeat through the night, I had to be intentional about not giving fear a place if I skipped a night. I'm so grateful for grace!

Right now, you may be thinking that this is too

hard and that not having a spelled-out step leaves too much margin for error. You may be saying to yourself that you can't hear the voice of the Lord. Stop! Take that thought captive! Do not miss the incredible opportunity you've been given to partner with the King of Heaven and earth! Let His perfect love for you cast out all the fear (and doubt) that is raging in your mind.

Give yourself permission to practice hearing and obeying the voice of the Lord. Don't worry about always getting it right. Remember, although people look at the outer things, God looks at the heart. He will reward, and if necessary, He will redirect a heart that desires to obey what He says. I would rather fail while earnestly trying to obey the Lord than succeed at being disobedient.

We are encouraged in Psalm 32:8. The Lord says, "I will guide you along the best pathway for your life. I will advise you and watch over you" (NLT). Here is the place where we hear God's will for the victory in our personal trials.

We are assured in Isaiah 30:20–21,

Though the Lord gave you adversity for food and suffering for drink, he will still be with you to teach you. You will see your teacher with your own eyes. Your own ears will hear him. Right behind you a voice will say, "This is the way you should go," whether to the right or to the left. (NLT)

Jesus promised us that His sheep would hear His voice (see John 10:27–28). The Passion Translation words it this way: "My own sheep will hear my voice and I know each one, and they will follow me. I give to them the gift of eternal life and they will never be lost and no one has the power to snatch them out of my hands." No one (and no circumstance) has the power to snatch you out of His hand.

I take very seriously the warning given to me in John 8:47. Jesus declares, "Anyone who belongs to God listens gladly to the words of God. But you don't listen because you don't belong to God."

I never want it said of me that I don't belong to

God. So while the things I am asked to do may seem awkward, weird, or even offensive, I want it to be said of me that I was obedient. I never want to dread this one-more-thing element or take it lightly, for this is where my trust in the Lord is solidified. No one else could bring about the miraculous things that I have witnessed with such seemingly inconsequential and irrelevant actions on my part. This is where His voice becomes personal and I feel His gaze fixed upon me.

I referenced Psalm 32:8 earlier in this chapter. The English Standard Version words it like this: "I will instruct you and teach you in the way you should go; *I will counsel you with my eye upon you*" (emphasis mine). This is the place where I get to see how true that is.

A Final Thought

There will come a time when the waiting is over, the miracle you've been praying for has become a reality, and you are standing in the fullness of your promise. From here, you can look back and see how the Lord has shown Himself faithful through every step of this journey. Even in the times when you felt alone and the place you were standing in seemed dark, you were able to see the evidence of His faithfulness and the truth of His promise to never leave you or forsake you.

Praise is coming forth from your lips, and you are ready to share your testimony with anyone who will listen. God never brings us from trial to triumph so that we will keep the victory to ourselves. You have been entrusted with shining His light and bring hope to those who are walking in fear and darkness.

It may not be right away, and it might not even be in the months immediately following, but I promise that sometime, somewhere, someone is going to need to lean on the strength of your victory, so be generous with what you have been given.

This probably doesn't come as a big shock to you. I was prepared and even excited to be used to bring hope to those who have suddenly found themselves ready to despair. But what I wasn't prepared for was letting go of the process.

It Was Never Meant to Last Forever

In this book, I've referenced several miracles that God has done in my life. Many and even most of these events happened in a relatively short span of time. It was so short, in fact, that I didn't even realize that I was walking any specific steps out on a regular basis. I just did what I knew to do and added any special instructions from the Lord that I received in that season. Afterward, I did my best to give Him glory and praise His name.

But then there are seasons that seem to go on forever. There are times when the miracle that we are believing for takes years and even decades to come to pass. Our commitment to walk out what we know on a daily basis takes the kind of faith that we probably don't even know that we have.

Do you remember when I told you about the miracle that took seven years? All that time, God was working to show me the power of praying His truth and speaking life and not death over what I was believing for. It was seven years of putting the armor of God on myself and my family regularly and daily refusing to keep any record of wrongs. It was holding fast for seven very long, scary, and uncertain years and believing deep in my heart that God was faithful, even when the thing that was in front of me seemed beyond restoration. It was being fully committed to go where He told me to go and pray what He told me to pray.

In this season, the steps became such a lifestyle for me that it slowly morphed into a habit. It was something that ended up defining my life and becoming part of my daily routine. I shared that the situation became very dark just weeks before the Lord brought the breakthrough. This stark contrast between darkness and His glorious light in such a short period became the catalyst for finally deciding to write this book. But when something has become part of your life for that long, and it has such emotion attached to it, it can be hard to let it go.

As the oppressiveness and urgency of our situation was gradually overtaken by hope and promise, I started to let go of the "daily-ness" of what I was doing. This is expected. After all, we are supposed to move from request to gratitude when God answers our prayers.

What I wasn't prepared for was the suffocating wave of fear that rushed in.

I had been doing these things for so long and focused so intently on what I needed God to do that I began to fear that the victory would somehow vanish or start to recede if I started to decrease what I had been doing.

How exhausting! We are always in a place of needing miracles in our lives. If we continue to follow each step, for every miracle that we are asking for as well as the ones that we have already received, we will never have time for anything else. At least, *I* believe that I need and receive so many miracles that this would be the case in my life.

I was unprepared for this feeling of fear. It was as if *my* actions had brought about the miracle in the first place. Remember in the beginning of this book how I said that we cannot *make* a miracle. We can only partner with the Giver of miracles and choose to bring our words and actions into alignment with Heaven, as we wait for God to move.

In what I would call *quick miracles*, it's easier to move from asking and believing to thanking and praising. But when I have to stand on the promises for years, it can become such a part of who I am and what I do that letting it go is like losing a piece of me.

I know that this is repetitive, but God is all

about relationship. I had to let Him do the work of reassuring me that He had in fact brought this miracle to completion. When the enemy's words of fear, doubt, and accusation tried to take hold of me, I had to go and sit with the Holy Spirit and let the peace of His love wash over me. This wasn't easy, and it wasn't quick, but it was a necessary part of the process.

Some of you are praying for your prodigal to return. Maybe you are believing for your marriage to be restored. I'm sure there are several of you who are believing that you will finally be healed from something you have been battling for years or even decades. While I am confident that God is going to do a great and mighty work in your life as you begin to faithfully apply what He has had me share with you, I want to encourage you to trust Him with the timing. Trust that He will move at exactly the right time for maximum impact and lasting results. He will also show you when to shift from contending in faith and fervent prayer to declaring Him faithful and singing His praise. There will be a time to say, "It is done," and move on.

It's not a formula, it's a process. It's a privileged walk with the One who knows our every need and shed His blood for our every victory. We don't have to live continually in the place of anxious waiting. Choose instead to press in and enjoy the journey as you wait for God to move. Stand firm and find joy while you wait for your miracle.

Scriptures to Build Your Faith

The following is an extensive list of miracles mentioned in the Bible. While this is in no way an exhaustive list, it does offer us a glimpse of the variety of ways that the God of Heaven and earth invaded the lives and circumstances of the men and women that we read about in scripture. These men and women are just like you and me. My prayer is that this will expand your thinking as to what is possible and cause you to believe God for *big* things—seemingly impossible things. I encourage you to read each (or at least one from each category) of the many examples that I've provided for you and ask the Lord these questions.

1. How did this miracle defy physical boundaries or worldly perceptions of what was possible? How did God's Word trump the current reality?

2. What part did faith play in this miracle?

3. How does the Scripture, "What the enemy intends for evil, God will use for good" (Gen 50:20) apply in this situation?

Deliverance from Enemies

Gideon (Judges 6–7)

Elisha's servant (2 Kings 6:8–23)

Esther (Esther 2–9)

Jesus (Mathew 2:13; Luke 4:20–30; John 8:57–59; 10:22–420

Paul and Silas (Acts 16:23–34)

Deliverance from Evil Spirits

King Nebuchadnezzar delivered from the spirit of pride (Daniel 4:19–37)

King Saul delivered from tormenting spirits (1 Samuel 16:14–23)

Mary Magdalene delivered from seven spirits (Mark 16:9; Luke 8:2)

A slave girl delivered from the spirit of divination by the apostle Paul (Acts 16:16)

Restoration

Jacob restored to his brother Esau (Genesis 32:3–33:12)

Jesus declares the woman with the issue of blood clean and well. Because the whole town knew her as the women with the issue of blood, this declaration would have been paramount to her reentering society (Luke 8:43–48)

We see evidence of the woman at the well being restored to society. It is a miracle that her witness was even deemed credible, given the history and traditions of the day (John 4:7–30; 39–42).

After repentance, mourning, and fasting, we see King David restored in his relationship to the Lord (2 Samuel 12:1–25).

Salvation

People of Nineveh (Jonah 1–3)

Matthew and Zacchaeus (Luke 5:27–28; 19:1–10)

People of Samaria (John 4:39–42)

Cornelius and his household (Acts 10)

The jailer (Acts 16:25–34)

Provision

Elijah (1 Kings 17:1–16)

The people of Egypt and beyond (Genesis 25–57)

A donkey and a coin (Luke 19:28–35; Matthew 17:27)

The five thousand fed (John 6:1–13)

Safety

Rahab (Joshua 2; 6:25)

David (1 Samuel 19:11-18; 23:13-14)

Paul had several miraculous saves, but here are some of my favorites (2 Corinthians 11:24–27; Acts 28:1–6).

Miracles over the Elements of Nature

The sun (Joshua 10:12)

The waves (Matthew 8:23–27; Mark 4:35–41; Luke 8:22–25)

The water (Exodus 14:9–30; Joshua 3–4)

Overcoming Barrenness

Hannah (1 Samuel 1:2–2:21)

Sarah (Genesis 17:16; 21:2)

Rachel (Genesis 30:22)

Elizabeth (Luke 1:5–25)

Finding a Spouse

Isaac (Genesis 24:1–28)

Ruth (Ruth 2–4)

Physical Death

The widow's son (Luke 7:11–17)

Dry bones (Ezekiel 37)

Jairus's daughter (Mark 5:21–43; Luke 8:40–56)

Many saints (Matthew 27:52)

Questions for Group Discussion

1

1. Is the idea of speaking the Word of God over your situation new to you?

2. How would your life and more specifically your attitude change if you believed that the promises in scripture were true for you?

3. What's stopping you from searching the scriptures to see what God has to say about your specific situation? Will you ask Him and declare what He says in faith?

4. What experience has the prophetic played in your life? Whether it is positive or negative, are you willing to ask the Lord to give you an encouraging word through trustworthy men and women in your life?

2

1. How is your speaking life lining up with or conflicting with your prayer life?

2. What feelings arise when I tell you that your words will bring either death or life to your health, marriage, children, etc.? What areas of your life need the most change when it comes to the words that you speak?

3. Do you have at least one wise and trusted mentor who speaks life into your situation? If not, will you ask the Lord to show you someone who is trustworthy that can help you to change your speech so that it lines up with the Word of God?

4. I mentioned that I have been guilty of sharing my journey with friends and people whom I was comfortable with, instead of asking the Lord whom He had placed in my life to walk alongside me. Do you tend to surround yourself with people whom you are comfortable with and those who will sympathize with you? Have you

allowed the Lord to bring people into your life who will challenge you to go to the next level?

5. What part does music play in your day-to-day emotions? Are you listening to music solely for entertainment purposes, or do you have a playlist of songs that inspire you to believe God and His promises for you? If not, will you take time to make one?

3

1. Are you currently putting the armor of God on yourself daily? If not, why not? If you are, when or in what way have you noticed a difference in the way your day goes?

2. Take some time to search the scriptures for places where the individual pieces of God's armor are mentioned. What additional insight does this give you as to the protection that the Lord has provided?

3. If you are believing God for a miracle in your marriage, your children, or another believer, begin to put the armor of God upon them as well. While being careful to honor the privacy of the other person, share some of the changes you have observed.

4. If waging war in a spiritual battle seems scary to you, take time to pray as a group and ask God to bring you peace. Remember that He has already won the victory and given you a complete set of armor and everything you need to wage successful warfare. Ask Him to give you additional insight into this. You may need to search the scriptures for examples where the Lord went before people to fight the battle. It will give you courage to know that you are never walking into battle alone or defenseless. Discuss your findings with your group.

4

1. I shared a very important truth at the beginning of this chapter: offense is a spirit and is not a feeling. Is this new for you or something you are familiar with? Does

seeing it as a spirit that you are equipped to fight instead of a feeling that you are powerless to control help you? If it does, in what way is this true?

2. I share some stories from my life that led me to form some very unhealthy ways of dealing with the challenges and people in my life. Did this chapter highlight any lies that you may have believed that have set up negative patterns in how you deal with conflict?

3. Matthew 6:14-15 and 7:12 show how important it is to the Father that we forgive quickly, often, and completely. In what way(s) is this difficult for you?

4. I discuss the concept of picking up offenses on behalf of other people (specifically our children) and to place this offense upon them, causing them to have to battle against offense themselves, even when they are not initially offended. Do you have the tendency of becoming offended on behalf of others?

5. I told the story of how the Lord had set someone up ahead of time to walk with my family during a very difficult time. The enemy had worked overtime to bring division just hours before tragic events unfolded. Thinking back through the years, can you identify a time when this may have happened in your life?

6. One thing that has been a critical part of my journey toward healthy, lasting relationships and seeing the miraculous play out in many situations is learning if, when, and how to confront others when I am offended by something they have done. Taking the time to process the offense with the Lord *before* interacting with the offender has been imperative. How do you react when offended? Has it been successful in your confrontations?

7. I ended the chapter with words regarding the offenses that we often carry against our spouses. I am often shocked at how quickly and furiously the spirit of offense can come on me when it comes to my marriage.

Is this something you struggle with? What are some steps that will help you process these feelings in a way that will increase trust and connection in your marriage (or even in your closest relationships)?

5

1. How well would you have done in the *hold fast* seasons of waiting for a miracle?

2. In what ways does the Word of God give you strategies that help in your current season?

3. What example or exhortation can you hold onto in your current season of waiting? Remember that the stories in the Bible are examples and *not* exceptions. If God did it for another person, He will do it for you.

4. Is there anything that you can do to build up your faith during this season of waiting? Sometimes reading a certain book, listening to a playlist, or finding like-minded friends to pray with regularly will help keep

us focused on our promise instead of our problem. While we should not strive to manipulate God, we are responsible for our attitude while we wait. Is there anything you can do to keep yourself full of faith?

6

1. Have you ever had an experience where you were sure that the Lord told you to do something that didn't seem to make sense in the moment? Did you do it?

2. How willing are you to appear undignified in your pursuit of God's favor and blessing in your life?

3. Many scriptures back up the truth that we can hear from the Lord. In fact, it is His deepest desire that we do so. If you struggle in this area, how do these scriptures help to increase your faith? Can you find other scriptures that support this?

4. How comfortable are you with being quiet before the Lord until He brings a strategy?

5. Remembering Psalm 32:8 ESV, how does it make you feel to know that the Lord is willing to counsel you with His eyes?

A Final Thought

1. Can you see yourself on the other side of your promise? Can you see yourself living in the days when the cry of your heart has been fulfilled? If you can, how hard do you imagine it will be to let go of the step-by-step processes and simply live in freedom? If you can't, are you willing to ask God to give you a dream or vision of what it will be like to live in the fulfillment of His promise?

To share how this book has impacted your life or to book Julianne to speak at an upcoming event, you can contact her at JulianneKingMinistries@gmail.com.